LATVIAN COOKBOOK

Traditional Authentic Recipes from Latvia

LIAM LUXE

Copyright © 2023 Liam Luxe

All rights reserved.

CONTENTS

INTRODUCTION i
APPETIZERS AND STARTERS 1
   Sklandrausis (Carrot and Potato Pie) 1
   Rasols (Potato Salad) 2
   Siļķe ar biezpienu (Herring with Cottage Cheese) 3
   Aukstā zupa (Cold Beet Soup) 4
SOUPS AND BROTHS 6
   Zirņu zupa (Pea Soup) 6
   Biešu zupa (Beet Soup) 7
   Sorrel Soup (Skābeņu zupa) 8
   Lohikeitto (Salmon Soup) 10
   Dārzeņu zupa (Vegetable Soup) 11
SALADS AND SIDES 13
   Rupjmaize (Dark Rye Bread) 13
   Saldskābā kāpostu zupa (Sauerkraut Soup) 15
   Cepti kartupeļi (Roasted Potatoes) 16
   Grauzdiņi (Barley Porridge) 17
   Ķiploku maize (Garlic Bread) 18
MAIN COURSES 20
   Cepumi (Pork Roast) 20
   Teļa lielā fileja (Veal Cutlets) 21
   Kāposts ar desu (Cabbage Rolls with Meat) 23
   Zandartēts (Zander Fillet) 24

Skabētu zivju mērce (Sour Fish Sauce) 26

BREADS AND PASTRIES 28

Pīrāgi (Bacon Buns) 28

Siers kūka (Cheese Pie) 30

Ķimeņmaize (Caraway Rye Bread) 32

Cepumi (Latvian Cookies) 34

Maizes zupa (Bread Soup) 35

DESSERTS AND SWEET TREATS 38

Rupjmaizes kartupelis (Rye Bread Pudding) 38

Sklandrausis (Sweet Carrot Pie) 39

Saldējums (Latvian Ice Cream) 42

Medus kūka (Honey Cake) 44

Ķirbju pīrāgs (Pumpkin Pie) 46

HOLIDAY SPECIALTIES 50

Jāņi Cheese (Farmhouse Cheese) 50

Ziemassvētku kāposti (Christmas Sauerkraut) 53

Pīrāgi (Holiday Bacon Buns) 55

Svētku maize (Rye Bread for Festivals) 57

VEGETARIAN AND VEGAN DISHES 60

Sēņu biešu zupa (Mushroom Beet Soup) 60

Sierputra (Cottage Cheese Porridge) 62

Vegetārais pīrāgs (Vegetable Pie) 63

Biezpiena plācenīši (Cottage Cheese Pancakes) 65

Vegetable Stir-Fry 67

TIME-HONORED FAVORITES 70

Kartupeļu pankūkas (Potato Pancakes) 70

    Karbonāde (Pork Schnitzel) 72
    Ķoņi (Cabbage and Pork Stew) 73
    Melnie zirņi ar speķi (Black Peas with Bacon) 75
    Raugi (Dill-Pickled Cucumbers) 77
SPECIAL OCCASION CAKES 80
    Mierīgā torte (Peace Cake) 80
    Lāčplēša dienas kūka (Independence Day Cake) 82
    Bumbieru torte (Pear Cake) 85
    Medus kūka (Honey Cake) 88
    Sarkanāsku torte (Red Currant Cake) 91
PIES AND TARTS 94
    Ābolu pīrāgs (Apple Pie) 94
    Riekstu pīrāgs (Nut Tart) 97
    Ķirbju pīrāgs (Pumpkin Pie) 99
    Rabarberu pīrāgs (Rhubarb Pie) 102
    Ķimeņmaizes pīrāgs (Caraway Seed Pie) 104
MEASUREMENT CONVERSIONS 107

INTRODUCTION

This is a book full of tasty recipes from Latvia. You'll learn how to make Latvian food, from easy starters to yummy desserts. Whether you're new to cooking or a pro in the kitchen, the recipes are simple to follow.

APPETIZERS AND STARTERS

SKLANDRAUSIS (CARROT AND POTATO PIE)

Servings: 6-8 **Time:** 2 hours

Ingredients:

- 2 cups grated potatoes
- 1 cup grated carrots
- 1 cup rye flour
- 2 tbsp sugar
- 2 tbsp sour cream
- 1/2 tsp salt
- 1/2 tsp caraway seeds
- 1/2 tsp ground cinnamon

Instructions:

1. **Prepare the Filling:** In a mixing bowl, combine the grated potatoes and carrots. Add sugar, salt, caraway seeds, and cinnamon. Mix well.
2. **Make the Dough:** In a separate bowl, combine the rye flour and sour cream. Mix until a dough forms.
3. **Assemble the Pies:** Take small portions of the dough and roll them into balls. Flatten each ball into a thin, round dough circle. Place a spoonful of the potato and carrot filling in the center of the dough circle.
4. **Shape the Pies:** Fold the edges of the dough circle over the filling to create a round pie. Use a fork to crimp the edges and seal the pie.
5. **Bake:** Preheat your oven to 180°C (350°F). Place the sklandrausis on a baking sheet and bake for about 30-35 minutes, or until they turn golden brown.
6. **Serve:** Let the sklandrausis cool for a few minutes before serving. They can be enjoyed warm or at room temperature as an appetizer or snack.

RASOLS (POTATO SALAD)

Servings: 6-8 **Time:** 30 minutes

Ingredients:

- 4 medium potatoes, boiled and diced
- 3 hard-boiled eggs, chopped
- 2 pickles, diced
- 1/2 cup cooked peas
- 1/2 cup cooked carrots, diced
- 1/2 cup cooked beets, diced

- 1 small onion, finely chopped
- 1/2 cup mayonnaise
- 1/2 cup sour cream
- Salt and pepper, to taste

Instructions:

1. **Prepare the Ingredients:** Start by boiling the potatoes, eggs, peas, carrots, and beets until they're tender. Once they're cooked, dice the potatoes, chop the eggs, and dice the pickles, carrots, and beets.
2. **Mix the Vegetables:** In a large bowl, combine the diced potatoes, hard-boiled eggs, pickles, peas, carrots, beets, and finely chopped onion.
3. **Make the Dressing:** In a separate bowl, mix the mayonnaise and sour cream. Season with salt and pepper to taste.
4. **Combine and Chill:** Pour the dressing over the mixed vegetables and gently toss until everything is well coated.
5. **Chill and Serve:** Cover the bowl and refrigerate the potato salad for at least an hour to allow the flavors to meld. Serve chilled as a refreshing appetizer or side dish.

SIĻĶE AR BIEZPIENU (HERRING WITH COTTAGE CHEESE)

Servings: 4 **Time:** 20 minutes

Ingredients:

- 4 herring fillets, pickled or salted
- 1 cup cottage cheese

- 2 boiled eggs, finely chopped
- 1 small red onion, finely chopped
- 2 tablespoons sour cream
- 2 tablespoons fresh dill, chopped
- Salt and black pepper, to taste

Instructions:

1. **Prepare the Herring:** If your herring fillets are salted or pickled, rinse them in cold water to remove excess salt. Pat them dry with a paper towel.
2. **Prepare the Cottage Cheese Mixture:** In a bowl, combine the cottage cheese, chopped boiled eggs, finely chopped red onion, and fresh dill. Mix well. Season with a pinch of salt and a dash of black pepper.
3. **Assemble the Dish:** On individual plates, place a herring fillet. Top each herring fillet with a generous spoonful of the cottage cheese mixture.
4. **Garnish:** Drizzle a dollop of sour cream over the cottage cheese mixture, and sprinkle some extra chopped dill for garnish.
5. **Serve:** Siļķe ar biezpienu is best served chilled.

AUKSTĀ ZUPA (COLD BEET SOUP)

Servings: 4-6 **Time:** 30 minutes

Ingredients:

- 2 cups boiled and peeled beets, finely grated
- 2 cups kefir (fermented milk)
- 1 cucumber, finely diced
- 2 hard-boiled eggs, chopped

- 2-3 green onions, thinly sliced
- 2-3 radishes, thinly sliced
- 2 tablespoons fresh dill, chopped
- 1 tablespoon fresh chives, chopped
- 1 tablespoon white vinegar
- 1 teaspoon sugar
- Salt and black pepper, to taste
- Ice cubes (for serving)

Instructions:

1. **Prepare the Beets:** Boil the beets until tender, peel them, and finely grate them. Allow them to cool to room temperature.
2. **Mix the Soup Base:** In a large bowl, combine the grated beets and kefir. Stir until well combined.
3. **Season the Soup:** Add the white vinegar, sugar, and a pinch of salt and black pepper. Mix well and taste to adjust the seasonings as needed.
4. **Chill the Soup:** Cover the bowl and refrigerate the soup for at least an hour to let the flavors meld and to ensure it's nicely chilled.
5. **Serve:** When ready to serve, ladle the cold beet soup into individual bowls. Top each serving with diced cucumber, chopped hard-boiled eggs, sliced green onions, sliced radishes, fresh dill, and chives.
6. **Add Ice:** For an extra refreshing touch, you can add a couple of ice cubes to each bowl before serving.

SOUPS AND BROTHS

ZIRŅU ZUPA (PEA SOUP)

Servings: 4-6 **Time:** 1 hour

Ingredients:

- 1 cup dried green peas
- 1 onion, finely chopped
- 2 carrots, diced
- 2 potatoes, diced
- 4 cups vegetable or chicken broth
- 2-3 slices of bacon, chopped (optional)
- 1 bay leaf
- 2-3 sprigs of fresh parsley
- 1 tablespoon butter
- Salt and black pepper, to taste

Instructions:

1. **Prepare the Peas:** Rinse the dried green peas and soak them in cold water for a few hours or overnight. Drain before using.
2. **Sauté the Aromatics:** In a large pot, melt the butter over medium heat. If using bacon, cook it until it's crispy, then remove it from the pot. In the same pot, add the chopped onion and diced carrots. Sauté until the vegetables are soft and the onion is translucent.
3. **Cook the Soup:** Add the soaked and drained green peas to the pot. Pour in the vegetable or chicken broth. Drop in the bay leaf, and add the diced potatoes. Bring the mixture to a boil.
4. **Simmer:** Reduce the heat to a gentle simmer and cover the pot. Let the soup cook for about 40-45 minutes, or until the peas and vegetables are tender.
5. **Season:** Season the soup with salt and black pepper to taste. Remove the bay leaf.
6. **Serve:** Ladle the pea soup into bowls. If you cooked bacon earlier, you can sprinkle some of the crispy bacon bits on top for extra flavor. Garnish with fresh parsley.

BIEŠU ZUPA (BEET SOUP)

Servings: 4-6 **Time:** 1 hour

Ingredients:

- 3-4 medium beets, peeled and grated
- 1 large potato, peeled and diced
- 1 carrot, peeled and diced
- 1 onion, finely chopped

- 2 cups vegetable or chicken broth
- 1 bay leaf
- 2-3 tablespoons sour cream
- 1-2 teaspoons white vinegar
- Salt and black pepper, to taste
- Fresh dill, for garnish (optional)

Instructions:

1. **Prepare the Beets:** Peel the beets and grate them. If you don't want your hands to turn red, you can wear gloves during this process.
2. **Sauté the Aromatics:** In a large pot, sauté the finely chopped onion until it becomes translucent.
3. **Cook the Vegetables:** Add the grated beets, diced potato, and diced carrot to the pot. Stir well and cook for a few minutes.
4. **Add Broth and Bay Leaf:** Pour in the vegetable or chicken broth. Add the bay leaf for extra flavor. Bring the mixture to a boil.
5. **Simmer:** Reduce the heat, cover the pot, and simmer the soup for about 30-40 minutes, or until the vegetables are tender.
6. **Season and Serve:** Remove the bay leaf. Season the soup with salt and black pepper to taste. Stir in the sour cream and white vinegar.
7. **Garnish and Enjoy:** Ladle the beet soup into bowls. Garnish with fresh dill, if desired.

SORREL SOUP (SKĀBEŅU ZUPA)

Servings: 4-6 Time: 30 minutes

Ingredients:

- 4 cups sorrel leaves, washed and chopped
- 2 medium potatoes, peeled and diced
- 1 small onion, finely chopped
- 1 carrot, peeled and diced
- 1 celery stalk, diced
- 6 cups vegetable or chicken broth
- 2-3 tablespoons butter
- 2-3 tablespoons all-purpose flour
- 1/2 cup sour cream
- Salt and black pepper, to taste
- Fresh chives, for garnish (optional)

Instructions:

1. **Prepare the Sorrel:** Wash the sorrel leaves and chop them finely.
2. **Sauté the Aromatics:** In a large pot, melt the butter over medium heat. Add the finely chopped onion, diced carrot, and diced celery. Sauté until the vegetables are soft and the onion is translucent.
3. **Add Potatoes:** Add the diced potatoes to the pot and sauté for a few minutes.
4. **Simmer:** Pour in the vegetable or chicken broth and bring the mixture to a boil. Reduce the heat to a gentle simmer and cook for about 15-20 minutes, or until the potatoes are tender.
5. **Prepare the Roux:** In a separate pan, melt more butter over low heat. Stir in the flour to create a roux. Cook for a few minutes until the roux becomes lightly golden.
6. **Combine the Roux:** Gradually add the roux to the simmering soup, stirring constantly to avoid lumps.

7. **Add Sorrel:** Add the chopped sorrel leaves to the soup and continue to simmer for another 5-7 minutes, or until the sorrel wilts.
8. **Season:** Season the soup with salt and black pepper to taste.
9. **Serve:** Ladle the sorrel soup into bowls. Add a dollop of sour cream and garnish with fresh chives, if desired.

LOHIKEITTO (SALMON SOUP)

Servings: 4-6 **Time:** 30 minutes

Ingredients:

- 1 lb (450g) salmon fillet, skin removed and cut into bite-sized pieces
- 2 potatoes, peeled and diced
- 1 leek, washed and thinly sliced
- 1 carrot, peeled and diced
- 1 celery stalk, diced
- 4 cups fish or vegetable broth
- 1 cup heavy cream
- 1 bay leaf
- 2-3 tablespoons butter
- 2-3 tablespoons all-purpose flour
- 1/4 cup fresh dill, chopped
- Salt and black pepper, to taste
- Lemon wedges, for serving

Instructions:

1. **Sauté the Vegetables:** In a large pot, melt the butter over medium heat. Add the leek, carrot, and celery. Sauté

until the vegetables are tender and the leek is soft and translucent.
2. **Create a Roux:** Stir in the flour to create a roux. Cook for a few minutes until the roux becomes lightly golden.
3. **Add Broth and Potatoes:** Gradually pour in the fish or vegetable broth, stirring to combine with the roux. Add the diced potatoes and the bay leaf. Bring the mixture to a gentle simmer and cook for about 10-15 minutes, or until the potatoes are tender.
4. **Add Salmon:** Carefully add the bite-sized pieces of salmon to the simmering soup. Cook for 5-7 minutes, or until the salmon is opaque and flakes easily.
5. **Stir in Cream:** Pour in the heavy cream and stir to combine. Heat the soup without letting it boil.
6. **Season:** Season the soup with salt and black pepper to taste.
7. **Serve:** Ladle the salmon soup into bowls. Garnish with chopped fresh dill and serve with lemon wedges on the side.

DĀRZEŅU ZUPA (VEGETABLE SOUP)

Servings: 4-6 **Time:** 45 minutes

Ingredients:

- 1 onion, finely chopped
- 2 carrots, peeled and diced
- 2 potatoes, peeled and diced
- 1 parsnip, peeled and diced
- 1 celery stalk, diced
- 1/2 cup green beans, chopped
- 1/2 cup cauliflower florets

- 1/2 cup peas (fresh or frozen)
- 4 cups vegetable or chicken broth
- 2-3 tablespoons butter
- 2-3 tablespoons all-purpose flour
- 1 bay leaf
- 2-3 tablespoons fresh dill, chopped
- Salt and black pepper, to taste

Instructions:

1. **Sauté the Aromatics:** In a large pot, melt the butter over medium heat. Add the finely chopped onion, diced carrots, celery, parsnip, and potatoes. Sauté until the vegetables are soft and the onion is translucent.
2. **Create a Roux:** Stir in the flour to create a roux. Cook for a few minutes until the roux becomes lightly golden.
3. **Add Broth:** Gradually pour in the vegetable or chicken broth, stirring to combine with the roux. Add the bay leaf.
4. **Simmer:** Bring the mixture to a gentle simmer and cook for about 10-15 minutes, or until the vegetables are tender.
5. **Add Remaining Vegetables:** Add the green beans, cauliflower, and peas to the soup. Continue to simmer for an additional 10 minutes, or until these vegetables are tender.
6. **Season:** Season the soup with salt and black pepper to taste.
7. **Serve:** Ladle the vegetable soup into bowls. Garnish with chopped fresh dill.

SALADS AND SIDES

RUPJMAIZE (DARK RYE BREAD)

Servings: 1 loaf **Time:** 18-24 hours (including resting time)

Ingredients:

- 1 1/2 cups dark rye flour
- 1/2 cup whole wheat flour
- 1/2 cup all-purpose flour
- 1 1/2 cups lukewarm water
- 2 teaspoons salt
- 1 teaspoon sugar
- 1/2 packet (about 1/2 teaspoon) active dry yeast

Instructions:

1. **Mix the Yeast Starter:** In a small bowl, combine 1/2 cup of dark rye flour, 1/2 cup of lukewarm water, sugar, and yeast. Stir well and let it rest for about 10-15 minutes, or until it becomes frothy. This is your yeast starter.
2. **Combine Flours:** In a large mixing bowl, combine the remaining dark rye flour, whole wheat flour, all-purpose flour, and salt.
3. **Create the Dough:** Pour the yeast starter and the remaining 1 cup of lukewarm water into the flour mixture. Mix well until the dough comes together.
4. **Knead:** Turn the dough out onto a floured surface and knead it for about 10-15 minutes, or until it becomes smooth and elastic.
5. **First Rise:** Place the dough in a lightly oiled bowl, cover it with a clean kitchen towel, and let it rise for about 8-12 hours, or until it has doubled in size.
6. **Shape the Loaf:** After the first rise, remove the dough from the bowl and shape it into a round or oval loaf. Place it on a baking sheet lined with parchment paper.
7. **Second Rise:** Cover the loaf with a kitchen towel and let it rise for an additional 1-2 hours.
8. **Preheat Oven:** Preheat your oven to 220°C (430°F) and place a baking stone or an inverted baking sheet in the oven to preheat as well.
9. **Bake:** Just before baking, make a few slashes on the top of the loaf with a sharp knife. Transfer the loaf, with the parchment paper, onto the preheated baking stone or inverted baking sheet. Bake for about 30-40 minutes, or until the bread sounds hollow when tapped on the bottom.
10. **Cool:** Allow the rupjmaize to cool on a wire rack before slicing.

SALDSKĀBĀ KĀPOSTU ZUPA
(SAUERKRAUT SOUP)

Servings: 4-6 **Time:** 1 hour

Ingredients:

- 2 cups sauerkraut, drained and rinsed
- 1 onion, finely chopped
- 2 potatoes, peeled and diced
- 1 carrot, peeled and diced
- 1 celery stalk, diced
- 1/2 cup smoked sausage, sliced (optional)
- 4 cups vegetable or chicken broth
- 2-3 tablespoons butter
- 2-3 tablespoons all-purpose flour
- 1 bay leaf
- 1 teaspoon caraway seeds
- 1/2 cup sour cream
- Salt and black pepper, to taste
- Fresh dill, for garnish (optional)

Instructions:

1. **Sauté the Aromatics:** In a large pot, melt the butter over medium heat. Add the finely chopped onion, diced carrots, and celery. Sauté until the vegetables are soft and the onion is translucent.
2. **Create a Roux:** Stir in the flour to create a roux. Cook for a few minutes until the roux becomes lightly golden.
3. **Add Broth:** Gradually pour in the vegetable or chicken broth, stirring to combine with the roux. Add the bay leaf and caraway seeds.

4. **Simmer:** Bring the mixture to a gentle simmer and cook for about 15-20 minutes.
5. **Add Potatoes and Sauerkraut:** Add the diced potatoes and drained, rinsed sauerkraut to the soup. Simmer for another 15-20 minutes, or until the potatoes are tender.
6. **Sauté Sausage:** If using smoked sausage, sauté the slices in a separate pan until they are lightly browned.
7. **Season and Add Sausage:** Season the soup with salt and black pepper to taste. If you sautéed sausage, add it to the soup.
8. **Serve:** Ladle the sauerkraut soup into bowls. Add a dollop of sour cream and garnish with fresh dill, if desired.

CEPTI KARTUPEĻI (ROASTED POTATOES)

Servings: 4 Time: 45 minutes

Ingredients:

- 4-5 medium-sized potatoes, washed and cubed
- 2-3 tablespoons vegetable oil
- 2 cloves garlic, minced (optional)
- 1 teaspoon dried rosemary (or herbs of your choice)
- Salt and black pepper, to taste

Instructions:

1. **Preheat Oven:** Preheat your oven to 220°C (430°F).
2. **Prepare Potatoes:** Wash the potatoes thoroughly and cut them into bite-sized cubes. If you prefer, you can leave the skin on for added texture and flavor.

3. **Toss with Oil:** In a large mixing bowl, toss the potato cubes with vegetable oil. You can also add minced garlic for extra flavor, if desired.
4. **Season:** Season the potatoes with dried rosemary (or herbs of your choice), salt, and black pepper. Mix well to ensure even coating.
5. **Roast:** Spread the seasoned potatoes in a single layer on a baking sheet or roasting pan. Make sure they are not crowded, as this allows them to roast evenly.
6. **Bake:** Roast the potatoes in the preheated oven for about 30-40 minutes, or until they are crispy and golden brown. Stir the potatoes occasionally to ensure even cooking.
7. **Serve:** Remove the roasted potatoes from the oven and transfer them to a serving dish.

GRAUZDIŅI (BARLEY PORRIDGE)

Servings: 4-6 **Time:** 1.5 hours

Ingredients:

- 1 cup pearl barley
- 4 cups water
- 2 cups milk
- 1/4 cup heavy cream
- 2 tablespoons butter
- 1/4 cup sugar (adjust to taste)
- 1/2 teaspoon salt
- 1/2 teaspoon vanilla extract (optional)
- Ground cinnamon, for garnish (optional)

Instructions:

1. **Rinse and Soak:** Rinse the pearl barley under cold water until the water runs clear. In a bowl, soak the barley in 2 cups of water for about 2 hours. Drain the barley after soaking.
2. **Boil Barley:** In a large pot, combine the soaked barley and 4 cups of water. Bring it to a boil, then reduce the heat to a simmer. Cook for about 30-40 minutes or until the barley is tender, but not mushy. Drain any excess water.
3. **Add Milk:** Return the cooked barley to the pot. Add the 2 cups of milk and simmer over low heat. Stir frequently as it simmers to prevent sticking and to help thicken the porridge.
4. **Stir in Cream and Butter:** Once the mixture has thickened, stir in the heavy cream and butter. Continue to cook and stir until the mixture is creamy and the butter is fully incorporated.
5. **Sweeten and Flavor:** Add sugar and a pinch of salt to the porridge. Adjust the sugar to your taste. If desired, add a splash of vanilla extract for extra flavor.
6. **Serve:** Ladle the barley porridge into bowls. Garnish with a sprinkle of ground cinnamon, if desired.

ĶIPLOKU MAIZE (GARLIC BREAD)

Servings: 4-6 **Time:** 15 minutes

Ingredients:

- 1 loaf of crusty bread (such as baguette or French bread)
- 4-5 cloves of garlic, minced
- 1/2 cup (1 stick) unsalted butter, at room temperature

- 2 tablespoons fresh parsley, chopped
- Salt and black pepper, to taste

Instructions:

1. **Preheat Oven:** Preheat your oven to 180°C (350°F).
2. **Prepare Garlic Butter:** In a bowl, combine the minced garlic and softened unsalted butter. Mix until the garlic is evenly distributed throughout the butter. You can also add a pinch of salt and black pepper to taste.
3. **Slice Bread:** Slice the loaf of crusty bread in half lengthwise, creating two long pieces of bread.
4. **Spread Garlic Butter:** Spread the garlic and butter mixture evenly over the cut sides of the bread.
5. **Bake:** Place the garlic bread on a baking sheet, cut side up. Bake in the preheated oven for about 10-12 minutes, or until the bread is crispy and the garlic butter has melted and become fragrant.
6. **Garnish:** Sprinkle the fresh parsley over the garlic bread while it's still warm.
7. **Serve:** Slice the garlic bread into individual portions and serve immediately. Enjoy this simple and flavorful Latvian classic as a side dish or appetizer.

MAIN COURSES

CEPUMI (PORK ROAST)

Servings: 4-6 **Time:** 2 hours

Ingredients:

- 2.5 lbs (1.1 kg) boneless pork loin or shoulder
- 4 cloves garlic, minced
- 2 tablespoons Dijon mustard
- 2 tablespoons honey
- 2 tablespoons olive oil
- 2 tablespoons soy sauce
- 1 teaspoon dried thyme
- Salt and black pepper, to taste
- 1 cup chicken or vegetable broth
- 2-3 tablespoons all-purpose flour (for the gravy)

Instructions:

1. **Preheat Oven:** Preheat your oven to 180°C (350°F).
2. **Prepare the Pork:** Place the pork roast in a roasting pan or on a baking sheet with a wire rack. Make small slits or incisions all over the pork using a knife.
3. **Prepare the Marinade:** In a bowl, combine the minced garlic, Dijon mustard, honey, olive oil, soy sauce, dried thyme, salt, and black pepper. Mix well.
4. **Marinate the Pork:** Brush or rub the marinade evenly over the entire surface of the pork roast. Make sure to get the marinade into the slits or incisions. Allow the pork to marinate for at least 30 minutes, or you can refrigerate it for several hours or overnight for even more flavor.
5. **Roast the Pork:** Place the marinated pork roast in the preheated oven. Roast for about 1.5 to 2 hours or until the internal temperature reaches 70°C (160°F). Baste the pork with pan juices every 20-30 minutes for added moisture and flavor.
6. **Rest the Pork:** Remove the roasted pork from the oven and let it rest for about 10-15 minutes before slicing.
7. **Prepare Gravy:** While the pork is resting, you can make a gravy using the pan juices. In a saucepan, heat the pan juices, add flour, and whisk to make a roux. Gradually add the chicken or vegetable broth while continuing to whisk. Simmer until the gravy thickens, and season with salt and pepper to taste.
8. **Slice and Serve:** Slice the roasted pork and serve with the homemade gravy.

TEĻA LIELĀ FILEJA (VEAL CUTLETS)

Servings: 4-6 **Time:** 30-40 minutes

Ingredients:

- 4 veal cutlets (veal schnitzel)
- 1 cup all-purpose flour
- 2 eggs
- 1 cup breadcrumbs
- 2-3 tablespoons vegetable oil
- Salt and black pepper, to taste
- Lemon wedges, for serving (optional)

Instructions:

1. **Prep the Veal Cutlets:** If the veal cutlets are large, you can pound them to an even thickness of about 1/4 inch. Season them with salt and black pepper.
2. **Create a Breading Station:** Prepare three shallow dishes. In the first dish, place the flour. In the second dish, beat the eggs. In the third dish, place the breadcrumbs.
3. **Coat the Veal Cutlets:** Dredge each veal cutlet in the flour, making sure to shake off any excess. Dip it in the beaten eggs, allowing any excess to drip off. Finally, coat it with breadcrumbs, pressing the breadcrumbs onto the cutlet to adhere.
4. **Heat Oil:** In a large skillet, heat the vegetable oil over medium-high heat.
5. **Fry the Veal Cutlets:** Once the oil is hot, add the breaded veal cutlets to the skillet. Fry for about 2-3 minutes per side, or until they are golden brown and the veal is cooked through. The internal temperature should reach 70°C (160°F).

6. **Drain and Rest:** Place the cooked veal cutlets on a paper towel-lined plate to drain any excess oil. Allow them to rest for a couple of minutes.
7. **Serve:** Serve the veal cutlets hot, with lemon wedges on the side if desired.

KĀPOSTS AR DESU (CABBAGE ROLLS WITH MEAT)

Servings: 4-6 **Time:** 2 hours

Ingredients:

- 1 large head of cabbage
- 1 lb (450g) ground pork and beef mix
- 1 cup cooked rice
- 1 onion, finely chopped
- 2 cloves garlic, minced
- 1 egg
- 1/2 cup milk
- 1/4 cup fresh parsley, chopped
- 2 tablespoons butter
- 1 can (14 oz) diced tomatoes
- 2 tablespoons tomato paste
- 1 teaspoon paprika
- Salt and black pepper, to taste
- Sour cream, for serving (optional)

Instructions:

1. **Prepare the Cabbage Leaves:** Fill a large pot with water and bring it to a boil. Carefully add the whole head of cabbage and simmer for about 10-15 minutes, or until the

outer leaves become soft and pliable. Remove the cabbage from the pot, allow it to cool, and then carefully peel off the leaves. Cut out the thick stem from each leaf to make rolling easier.
2. **Make the Filling:** In a large mixing bowl, combine the ground pork and beef mix, cooked rice, finely chopped onion, minced garlic, egg, milk, and chopped parsley. Season with salt and black pepper. Mix well to create the filling.
3. **Assemble the Cabbage Rolls:** Place a spoonful of the meat and rice filling in the center of each cabbage leaf. Fold the sides over the filling, then roll up the leaf to encase the filling. Repeat for all the cabbage leaves.
4. **Prepare the Sauce:** In a large skillet or pot, melt the butter over medium heat. Stir in the diced tomatoes, tomato paste, paprika, and a bit of salt and black pepper. Simmer for a few minutes.
5. **Cook the Cabbage Rolls:** Place the cabbage rolls in the skillet with the sauce. Make sure they are snugly arranged. Cover the skillet and simmer for about 45-60 minutes, or until the cabbage is tender and the meat filling is fully cooked.
6. **Serve:** Serve the cabbage rolls hot, with a dollop of sour cream if desired.

ZANDARTĒTS (ZANDER FILLET)

Servings: 4 Time: 30 minutes

Ingredients:

- 4 zander fillets (about 6-8 ounces each), skin-on
- 1/4 cup all-purpose flour

- Salt and black pepper, to taste
- 2 tablespoons vegetable oil
- 1 lemon, thinly sliced
- 2-3 sprigs of fresh dill
- 1/2 cup white wine or fish stock
- 2 tablespoons butter
- Fresh dill, for garnish
- Lemon wedges, for serving

Instructions:

1. **Prep the Zander Fillets:** Pat the zander fillets dry with paper towels. Season both sides with salt and black pepper. Dredge the fillets in flour, shaking off any excess.
2. **Heat the Oil:** In a large skillet, heat the vegetable oil over medium-high heat.
3. **Sear the Fillets:** Once the oil is hot, add the zander fillets, skin-side down. Sear for about 3-4 minutes until the skin is crispy and golden brown. Carefully flip the fillets and sear the other side for an additional 3-4 minutes. The fish is done when it flakes easily and has a nice golden crust. Transfer the fillets to a plate and keep them warm.
4. **Add Lemon and Dill:** In the same skillet, add the lemon slices, fresh dill sprigs, and white wine (or fish stock). Simmer for a few minutes to reduce the liquid and infuse the flavors.
5. **Create a Sauce:** Stir in the butter to create a silky sauce. Season the sauce with a little more salt and black pepper if needed.
6. **Serve:** Place the zander fillets on serving plates. Pour the lemon and dill sauce over the fish. Garnish with fresh dill and serve with lemon wedges.

SKABĒTU ZIVJU MĒRCE (SOUR FISH SAUCE)

Servings: Makes about 1 cup **Time:** 15 minutes (plus marinating time)

Ingredients:

- 1 cup white fish fillets, such as pike or perch, cut into small pieces
- 1 small onion, finely chopped
- 1/4 cup water
- 1/4 cup white wine vinegar
- 1/4 cup sugar
- Salt, to taste
- Black pepper, to taste
- Fresh dill, for garnish (optional)

Instructions:

1. **Prepare the Fish:** In a bowl, combine the small pieces of white fish fillets with the finely chopped onion.
2. **Prepare the Marinade:** In a separate saucepan, combine the water, white wine vinegar, and sugar. Heat over medium heat, stirring until the sugar is dissolved. Bring the mixture to a boil.
3. **Marinate the Fish:** Pour the hot marinade over the fish and onions. Stir to combine. Season with salt and black pepper to taste. The fish should be fully submerged in the marinade.
4. **Marinating:** Cover the bowl and let the fish marinate in the refrigerator for at least 4-6 hours or, ideally,

overnight. The fish will become pickled and tender during this time.
5. **Serve:** When ready to serve, transfer the sour fish sauce to a serving dish. Garnish with fresh dill, if desired. It can be enjoyed as a side dish or condiment.

BREADS AND PASTRIES

PĪRĀGI (BACON BUNS)

Servings: Makes about 24 buns **Time:** 2-3 hours

Ingredients:

For the Dough:

- 4 cups all-purpose flour
- 1 cup warm milk
- 1/4 cup warm water
- 2 tablespoons sugar
- 2 1/4 teaspoons active dry yeast (1 packet)
- 1/4 cup melted butter
- 1 egg
- 1 teaspoon salt

For the Filling:

- 8 oz (225g) bacon, finely chopped
- 1 medium onion, finely chopped
- Salt and black pepper, to taste

For Brushing:

- 1 egg yolk, beaten

Instructions:

Preparing the Dough:

1. In a small bowl, combine warm water, warm milk, and sugar. Sprinkle the yeast over the mixture and let it sit for about 5-10 minutes, or until it becomes frothy.
2. In a large mixing bowl, combine the flour and salt. Make a well in the center.
3. Pour the yeast mixture, melted butter, and egg into the well. Mix everything together until a dough forms.
4. Knead the dough on a floured surface for about 5-7 minutes, or until it's smooth and elastic.
5. Place the dough in a lightly oiled bowl, cover it with a kitchen towel, and let it rise for about 1 hour, or until it has doubled in size.

Preparing the Filling:

1. In a skillet, cook the finely chopped bacon until it becomes crispy.

2. Remove the bacon from the skillet, leaving the bacon grease.
3. In the same skillet, sauté the finely chopped onion in the bacon grease until it becomes translucent.
4. Combine the cooked bacon and sautéed onions in a bowl. Season with salt and black pepper to taste.

Assembling the Pīrāgi:

1. Preheat your oven to 180°C (350°F).
2. Punch down the risen dough and divide it into two equal portions.
3. Roll out one portion of the dough into a thin rectangle on a floured surface.
4. Cut the rolled-out dough into squares, then place a spoonful of the bacon and onion filling in the center of each square.
5. Fold the dough over the filling to create a triangle shape, then pinch the edges to seal.
6. Place the filled pīrāgi on a baking sheet lined with parchment paper.
7. Repeat the process with the second portion of the dough.

Baking the Pīrāgi:

1. Brush the tops of the pīrāgi with beaten egg yolk.
2. Bake in the preheated oven for about 20-25 minutes, or until they are golden brown.
3. Remove from the oven and let them cool slightly before serving.

SIERS KŪKA (CHEESE PIE)

Servings: 8-10 **Time:** 1 hour

Ingredients:

For the Dough:

- 2 cups all-purpose flour
- 1/2 cup unsalted butter, cold and cubed
- 1/4 cup cold water
- 1/2 teaspoon salt

For the Filling:

- 2 cups cottage cheese (or farmer's cheese)
- 1/2 cup sour cream
- 1/2 cup granulated sugar
- 2 large eggs
- 1 teaspoon vanilla extract
- 1/4 cup raisins (optional)
- Zest of 1 lemon (optional)

For Dusting:

- Powdered sugar

Instructions:

Preparing the Dough:

1. In a food processor, combine the flour and cold, cubed butter. Pulse until the mixture resembles coarse crumbs.

2. With the food processor running, gradually add the cold water and salt. Process just until the dough comes together.
3. Turn the dough out onto a floured surface and knead it briefly to form a smooth ball. Wrap the dough in plastic wrap and refrigerate for at least 30 minutes.

Preparing the Filling:

1. In a bowl, combine the cottage cheese, sour cream, granulated sugar, eggs, and vanilla extract. Mix until the filling is smooth.
2. If desired, add raisins and lemon zest to the filling, stirring to combine.

Assembling the Siers kūka:

1. Preheat your oven to 180°C (350°F).
2. Roll out the chilled dough on a floured surface to fit a 9-inch pie dish.
3. Transfer the rolled-out dough to the pie dish, pressing it down to cover the bottom and sides.
4. Pour the cheese filling into the pie crust.
5. Bake in the preheated oven for about 35-40 minutes, or until the filling is set and the top is lightly golden.
6. Remove the pie from the oven and allow it to cool to room temperature.

Serving:

1. Once the Siers kūka has cooled, dust the top with powdered sugar.
2. Slice and serve this delightful Latvian Cheese Pie as a sweet and creamy dessert.

ĶIMEŅMAIZE (CARAWAY RYE BREAD)

Servings: 1 loaf **Time:** 3 hours (including rising time)

Ingredients:

- 2 cups rye flour
- 2 cups bread flour (or all-purpose flour)
- 1 1/2 cups warm water
- 1 packet (2 1/4 teaspoons) active dry yeast
- 2 teaspoons salt
- 1 tablespoon caraway seeds
- 1 tablespoon molasses (optional)
- Cornmeal (for dusting)
- Olive oil (for greasing)

Instructions:

1. **Activate the Yeast:** In a small bowl, combine the warm water, yeast, and molasses (if using). Let it sit for about 5-10 minutes until it becomes frothy.
2. **Mix the Flours:** In a large mixing bowl, combine the rye flour, bread flour, salt, and caraway seeds.
3. **Combine the Ingredients:** Pour the activated yeast mixture into the bowl with the dry ingredients. Mix everything together until a sticky dough forms.
4. **Knead the Dough:** Turn the dough out onto a well-floured surface. Knead the dough for about 10-15 minutes, or until it becomes smooth and elastic.
5. **Rise the Dough:** Place the dough in a greased bowl and cover it with a kitchen towel. Allow it to rise in a warm place for about 1-2 hours, or until it has doubled in size.

6. **Preheat Oven:** Preheat your oven to 200°C (390°F). Place a baking stone or a heavy baking sheet in the oven to heat up.
7. **Shape the Loaf:** Punch down the risen dough and shape it into a round or oval loaf. Place the loaf on a baking sheet or pizza peel that has been dusted with cornmeal.
8. **Second Rise:** Allow the shaped loaf to rise for another 30 minutes while the oven is preheating.
9. **Bake:** Score the top of the loaf with a sharp knife or razor blade. Slide the loaf onto the preheated baking stone or baking sheet. Bake for about 35-40 minutes, or until the bread is golden brown and sounds hollow when tapped on the bottom.
10. **Cool:** Transfer the baked bread to a wire rack and allow it to cool completely before slicing.

CEPUMI (LATVIAN COOKIES)

Servings: About 24 cookies **Time:** 45 minutes

Ingredients:

- 1/2 cup (1 stick) unsalted butter, at room temperature
- 1/2 cup granulated sugar
- 1 large egg
- 1 teaspoon vanilla extract
- 2 cups all-purpose flour
- 1 teaspoon baking powder
- A pinch of salt
- Zest of 1 lemon (optional)
- 1-2 tablespoons milk (if needed)
- Powdered sugar (for dusting)

Instructions:

1. **Preheat Oven:** Preheat your oven to 180°C (350°F). Line a baking sheet with parchment paper.
2. **Cream Butter and Sugar:** In a mixing bowl, cream together the room-temperature butter and granulated sugar until light and fluffy.
3. **Add Egg and Flavoring:** Beat in the egg and vanilla extract. If desired, add lemon zest for a hint of citrus flavor.
4. **Combine Dry Ingredients:** In a separate bowl, whisk together the all-purpose flour, baking powder, and a pinch of salt.
5. **Mix Dough:** Gradually add the dry ingredients to the wet mixture. Mix until a smooth cookie dough forms. If the dough is too crumbly, you can add a tablespoon or two of milk to help it come together.
6. **Shape Cookies:** Roll the dough into small balls (about 1 inch in diameter) and place them on the prepared baking sheet, leaving some space between each.
7. **Flatten Cookies:** Use a fork to gently flatten each cookie, creating a crisscross pattern on top.
8. **Bake:** Place the baking sheet in the preheated oven and bake for about 10-12 minutes, or until the cookies are just starting to turn golden at the edges.
9. **Cool:** Remove the cookies from the oven and let them cool on a wire rack.
10. **Dust with Powdered Sugar:** Once the cookies are completely cool, dust them with powdered sugar.

MAIZES ZUPA (BREAD SOUP)

Servings: 4-6 **Time:** 30 minutes

Ingredients:

- 4-6 slices of Latvian rye bread (or any dense rye bread)
- 4 cups water
- 1/2 cup heavy cream
- 1/4 cup sugar
- 1/4 cup butter
- 1/4 cup raisins
- 1/4 teaspoon ground cinnamon
- 1/4 teaspoon vanilla extract (optional)

Instructions:

1. **Tear Bread:** Tear the rye bread into bite-sized pieces and place them in a large mixing bowl.
2. **Boil Water:** In a large saucepan, bring 4 cups of water to a boil.
3. **Pour Boiling Water:** Pour the boiling water over the torn rye bread. Let it sit for about 10-15 minutes, allowing the bread to soften and break down.
4. **Blend or Mash:** Using a hand blender or a potato masher, blend the soaked bread until it becomes a smooth, porridge-like consistency.
5. **Sweeten and Flavor:** Return the mixture to low heat. Stir in the sugar, butter, raisins, ground cinnamon, and vanilla extract (if using). Mix well, allowing the butter to melt and the sugar to dissolve. Simmer for a few more minutes to incorporate the flavors.
6. **Add Cream:** Stir in the heavy cream, and simmer for another 2-3 minutes, ensuring it's well combined.

7. **Serve:** Maizes zupa can be served hot or cold. It's often enjoyed as a sweet dessert or a comforting snack.

DESSERTS AND SWEET TREATS

RUPJMAIZES KARTUPELIS (RYE BREAD PUDDING)

Servings: 4-6 **Time:** 1 hour

Ingredients:

- 6 slices of Latvian rye bread (or any dense rye bread)
- 2 cups whole milk
- 3/4 cup granulated sugar
- 2 eggs
- 1/4 cup unsalted butter, melted
- 1/4 cup raisins
- 1 teaspoon ground cinnamon
- 1/2 teaspoon vanilla extract (optional)

Instructions:

1. **Prepare Bread:** Tear the rye bread into bite-sized pieces and place them in a large mixing bowl.
2. **Soak Bread:** In a separate saucepan, heat the milk until it's hot but not boiling. Pour the hot milk over the torn rye bread. Let it sit for about 10-15 minutes to soften and absorb the milk.
3. **Preheat Oven:** Preheat your oven to 180°C (350°F). Grease a baking dish.
4. **Blend or Mash:** Using a hand blender or a potato masher, blend the soaked bread until it becomes a smooth, porridge-like consistency.
5. **Sweeten and Flavor:** In a separate bowl, whisk together the granulated sugar, eggs, melted butter, raisins, ground cinnamon, and vanilla extract (if using).
6. **Combine Mixtures:** Combine the sweetened mixture with the blended bread mixture. Mix well, ensuring that all ingredients are evenly distributed.
7. **Bake:** Pour the mixture into the greased baking dish. Bake in the preheated oven for about 30-40 minutes, or until the pudding is set and the top is golden brown.
8. **Serve:** Rupjmaizes kartupelis is typically served warm and can be enjoyed as a comforting dessert or snack.

SKLANDRAUSIS (SWEET CARROT PIE)

Servings: 8-10 **Time:** 2 hours

Ingredients:

For the Dough:

- 2 cups all-purpose flour
- 1/2 cup butter, cold and cubed
- 1/2 cup sour cream
- 1/4 teaspoon salt

For the Carrot Filling:

- 2 cups grated carrots
- 1/2 cup granulated sugar
- 1/2 teaspoon ground cinnamon
- 1/4 teaspoon ground cloves
- 1/4 teaspoon ground cardamom
- 1/4 teaspoon vanilla extract (optional)

For the Topping:

- 1/2 cup heavy cream
- 2 tablespoons granulated sugar

Instructions:

Preparing the Dough:

1. In a large mixing bowl, combine the all-purpose flour and salt.
2. Using a pastry cutter or your fingers, cut the cold, cubed butter into the flour until the mixture resembles coarse crumbs.
3. Stir in the sour cream and mix until a dough forms. If needed, add a little more sour cream to bring the dough together.
4. Divide the dough in half and shape each half into a disc. Wrap them in plastic wrap and refrigerate for at least 30 minutes.

Preparing the Carrot Filling:

1. In a bowl, combine the grated carrots, granulated sugar, ground cinnamon, ground cloves, ground cardamom, and vanilla extract (if using). Mix well and let it sit for about 15-20 minutes to allow the flavors to meld.

Assembling Sklandrausis:

1. Preheat your oven to 180°C (350°F).
2. Take one disc of dough and roll it out on a floured surface to fit the base of a 9-inch pie dish.
3. Place the rolled-out dough in the pie dish.
4. Spread the prepared carrot filling evenly over the dough.
5. Roll out the second disc of dough to create the top crust. You can cut strips or shapes from the dough to create a lattice or design on top of the filling.
6. Place the dough over the carrot filling, sealing the edges.

For the Topping:

1. In a small bowl, whisk together the heavy cream and granulated sugar.
2. Drizzle the cream mixture over the top crust.

Bake:

1. Place the Sklandrausis in the preheated oven and bake for about 45-50 minutes, or until the top is golden brown and the carrot filling is set.

2. Remove from the oven and let it cool before slicing and serving.

SALDĒJUMS (LATVIAN ICE CREAM)

Servings: 4-6 **Time:** Varies (accounting for ice cream machine and freezing)

Ingredients:

For the Ice Cream Base:

- 2 cups heavy cream
- 1 cup whole milk
- 1 cup granulated sugar
- 1 teaspoon vanilla extract
- 5 large egg yolks

For Flavor Variations (Optional):

- Fresh berries, chocolate chips, or your choice of mix-ins

Instructions:

Preparing the Ice Cream Base:

1. In a saucepan, combine the heavy cream and whole milk. Heat the mixture over medium heat until it's hot but not boiling. Remove it from the heat and stir in the vanilla extract.

2. In a separate bowl, whisk together the egg yolks and granulated sugar until the mixture is pale and creamy.
3. Gradually pour the hot milk and cream mixture into the egg yolk mixture, whisking continuously.
4. Return the combined mixture to the saucepan and cook over low heat, stirring constantly, until it thickens and coats the back of a spoon. This forms the custard base for your ice cream. Be careful not to let it boil.
5. Once thickened, remove the custard from heat and allow it to cool to room temperature. Then, refrigerate it for several hours or until it's thoroughly chilled.

Churning the Ice Cream:

1. Once the ice cream base is chilled, pour it into an ice cream maker and churn according to the manufacturer's instructions. This usually takes about 20-30 minutes.

Adding Mix-Ins (Optional):

1. If you want to add any flavor variations like fresh berries or chocolate chips, fold them into the ice cream just before transferring it to a lidded container for freezing.

Freezing the Ice Cream:

1. Transfer the churned ice cream to a lidded container and place it in the freezer for at least 3-4 hours or until it's firm.

Serving:

1. Scoop and serve the homemade Saldējums in bowls or cones.

MEDUS KŪKA (HONEY CAKE)

Servings: 12-16 **Time:** 3 hours (including chilling time)

Ingredients:

For the Cake Layers:

- 2 cups all-purpose flour
- 1/2 cup granulated sugar
- 1/4 cup unsalted butter, at room temperature
- 2 large eggs
- 1 teaspoon baking powder
- 1/2 teaspoon baking soda
- 1/4 teaspoon salt
- 1 teaspoon ground cinnamon
- 1/4 teaspoon ground cloves
- 1/4 teaspoon ground nutmeg
- 1/4 cup sour cream

For the Honey Filling:

- 1 cup honey
- 1/2 cup granulated sugar
- 1/2 cup unsalted butter
- 1/4 cup heavy cream
- 1/4 teaspoon salt
- 1 teaspoon vanilla extract

For the Cream Filling:

- 2 cups heavy cream
- 2 tablespoons powdered sugar
- 1 teaspoon vanilla extract

Instructions:

Preparing the Cake Layers:

1. Preheat your oven to 180°C (350°F). Grease and flour a 9x13-inch baking pan.
2. In a large mixing bowl, combine the flour, granulated sugar, baking powder, baking soda, salt, cinnamon, cloves, and nutmeg.
3. Add the softened butter and eggs. Mix well until the dough comes together.
4. Stir in the sour cream to create a soft, pliable dough.
5. Divide the dough into 8 equal portions and roll each portion into a ball.
6. Roll out each ball of dough into a thin layer (about the size of your baking pan) on a floured surface. Transfer the rolled-out dough to the prepared pan.
7. Bake each layer for about 5-6 minutes, or until they turn golden. You may need to bake them in batches.
8. Allow the cake layers to cool completely.

Preparing the Honey Filling:

1. In a saucepan, combine the honey, granulated sugar, butter, heavy cream, and salt. Bring the mixture to a boil while stirring constantly.
2. Reduce the heat to a simmer and cook for about 5-7 minutes, or until the mixture thickens slightly.

3. Remove from heat and stir in the vanilla extract. Let the honey filling cool to room temperature.

Preparing the Cream Filling:

1. In a mixing bowl, beat the heavy cream, powdered sugar, and vanilla extract until stiff peaks form.

Assembling the Medus kūka:

1. Place one cake layer on a serving platter. Spread a portion of the honey filling evenly over it.
2. Place another cake layer on top and repeat with the honey and cream fillings. Continue layering the cake and fillings until all the layers are used.
3. Finish with a layer of honey filling on top.
4. Use any remaining cream filling to frost the sides of the cake.
5. Refrigerate the cake for several hours or overnight to allow the flavors to meld and the cake to soften.

Serving:

1. Slice and serve the chilled Medus kūka. It's even better the next day!

ĶIRBJU PĪRĀGS (PUMPKIN PIE)

Servings: 8-10 **Time:** 2 hours (including chilling and baking)

Ingredients:

For the Pie Crust:

- 1 1/4 cups all-purpose flour
- 1/2 teaspoon salt
- 1/2 cup unsalted butter, cold and cubed
- 3-4 tablespoons ice water

For the Pumpkin Filling:

- 2 cups pumpkin puree (canned or homemade)
- 3/4 cup granulated sugar
- 1/2 teaspoon salt
- 1 teaspoon ground cinnamon
- 1/2 teaspoon ground ginger
- 1/4 teaspoon ground cloves
- 1/4 teaspoon ground nutmeg
- 2 large eggs
- 1 cup heavy cream

Instructions:

Preparing the Pie Crust:

1. In a mixing bowl, combine the all-purpose flour and salt.
2. Add the cold, cubed butter to the flour mixture. Use a pastry cutter or your fingers to cut the butter into the flour until the mixture resembles coarse crumbs.
3. Gradually add ice water, one tablespoon at a time, and mix until the dough comes together. Be careful not to overwork the dough.
4. Shape the dough into a disk, wrap it in plastic wrap, and refrigerate for at least 30 minutes.

Rolling Out the Crust:

1. Preheat your oven to 200°C (400°F).
2. On a floured surface, roll out the chilled dough into a circle to fit a 9-inch pie dish.
3. Carefully transfer the rolled-out dough to the pie dish, pressing it down to fit.
4. Trim any excess dough from the edges and create a decorative rim if desired.

Preparing the Pumpkin Filling:

1. In a mixing bowl, combine the pumpkin puree, granulated sugar, salt, ground cinnamon, ground ginger, ground cloves, and ground nutmeg.
2. Beat in the eggs until well combined.
3. Stir in the heavy cream.

Filling the Pie:

1. Pour the pumpkin filling into the prepared pie crust.
2. Smooth the top with a spatula.

Baking the Pie:

1. Place the pie in the preheated oven and bake for about 15 minutes.
2. Reduce the oven temperature to 180°C (350°F) and continue baking for an additional 35-40 minutes, or until the filling is set.
3. To check for doneness, insert a knife or toothpick into the center of the pie; it should come out clean when the pie is done.
4. Remove the pie from the oven and let it cool to room temperature.

Serving:

1. Slice and serve the Ķirbju pīrāgs as a delightful dessert, and you can also top it with whipped cream.

HOLIDAY SPECIALTIES

JĀṆI CHEESE (FARMHOUSE CHEESE)

Servings: Varies **Time:** 1 day

Ingredients:

- 4 liters of fresh cow's milk (can use whole milk)
- 1/2 teaspoon calcium chloride (optional, for better curd formation)
- 1/4 tablet of rennet or 1/4 teaspoon liquid rennet
- 1/4 cup cultured buttermilk (optional, for added tanginess)
- Salt to taste
- Cheese cloth

Instructions:

1. Prepare the Milk:

- If using fresh, unpasteurized milk, heat it to 37-40°C (98-104°F) in a large pot. If using pasteurized milk, add calcium chloride for better curd formation, then heat to the same temperature.

2. Add Rennet:

- Dissolve the rennet tablet or liquid rennet in a small amount of cool, non-chlorinated water.
- Stir this rennet solution into the warm milk.

3. Allow Curd Formation:

- Cover the milk and let it sit undisturbed for about 60-90 minutes to allow the curds to form. You'll know it's ready when you can make a clean break with a knife.

4. Cut Curds:

- Cut the curds into small cubes using a long knife.

5. Cook the Curds:

- Slowly heat the curds to 45-48°C (113-118°F) over the course of about 30-45 minutes. Stir gently to prevent sticking.

6. Drain and Rest:

- Once the curds have reached the desired temperature, remove them from the heat and let them sit for a few minutes to firm up.

- Line a colander with cheesecloth and pour the curds and whey through it. Allow the whey to drain off.

7. Add Buttermilk (Optional):

- If you wish to add extra tanginess, mix 1/4 cup of cultured buttermilk into the curds. This step is optional.

8. Form and Press:

- Gather the corners of the cheesecloth and twist to form a cheese bundle.
- Place the bundle in a cheese press and apply pressure for 6-8 hours, or until the cheese reaches your desired consistency.

9. Salt the Cheese:

- Remove the cheese from the press and sprinkle it with salt. Rub the salt into the cheese.

10. Age the Cheese:

- Place the cheese in a cool, dark place (around 10-15°C or 50-59°F) to age for at least 2 weeks. Turn it regularly to ensure even aging.

11. Enjoy:

- Once the Jāņi Cheese has aged to your liking, slice it and enjoy. It's perfect for a Jāņi celebration or any special occasion.

ZIEMASSVĒTKU KĀPOSTI (CHRISTMAS SAUERKRAUT)

Servings: 6-8 **Time:** 2 hours

Ingredients:

- 1 large head of sauerkraut (about 1.5 kg or 3.3 lbs)
- 1 large onion, finely chopped
- 2-3 cloves garlic, minced
- 2 tablespoons vegetable oil
- 1 teaspoon caraway seeds
- 1 bay leaf
- 1 teaspoon sugar
- 1/2 cup water
- Salt and pepper to taste
- Sour cream for serving (optional)

Instructions:

1. Rinse the Sauerkraut:

- Begin by rinsing the sauerkraut thoroughly under cold running water to remove some of the excess saltiness. Drain and set it aside.

2. Sauté Onions and Garlic:

- In a large pot, heat the vegetable oil over medium heat. Add the finely chopped onion and minced garlic. Sauté until they become translucent.

3. Add Sauerkraut:

- Add the rinsed sauerkraut to the pot and stir to combine with the onions and garlic.

4. Season and Cook:

- Season the sauerkraut mixture with caraway seeds, the bay leaf, sugar, salt, and pepper. Stir well to evenly distribute the flavors.

5. Add Water:

- Pour in the water to the pot. This will help the sauerkraut cook and become tender.

6. Simmer:

- Cover the pot and reduce the heat to low. Let the sauerkraut simmer for about 1.5 to 2 hours, or until it's tender and has absorbed the flavors.

7. Stir Occasionally:

- Stir the sauerkraut occasionally to prevent it from sticking to the bottom of the pot.

8. Taste and Adjust:

- Taste the sauerkraut and adjust the seasonings if needed. You can add a bit more salt, sugar, or caraway seeds to suit your preferences.

9. Serve:

- Remove the bay leaf and serve the Ziemassvētku kāposti hot. You can serve it as a side dish alongside traditional Latvian Christmas dishes.

Optional:

- Some people like to serve Ziemassvētku kāposti with a dollop of sour cream on top for extra creaminess and flavor.

PĪRĀGI (HOLIDAY BACON BUNS)

Servings: 24 buns **Time:** 2-3 hours

Ingredients:

For the Dough:

- 4 cups all-purpose flour
- 1 teaspoon salt
- 2 teaspoons sugar
- 1 cup warm milk
- 1/2 cup unsalted butter, melted
- 2 large eggs
- 2 1/4 teaspoons active dry yeast

For the Filling:

- 200g (7 oz) bacon, finely chopped
- 1 large onion, finely chopped
- 1 tablespoon butter
- Salt and pepper to taste

For the Egg Wash:

- 1 egg, beaten

Instructions:

Making the Dough:

1. In a small bowl, combine the warm milk, sugar, and yeast. Let it sit for about 5-10 minutes, or until it becomes frothy.
2. In a large mixing bowl, combine the flour and salt. Make a well in the center and add the melted butter, eggs, and the yeast mixture.
3. Mix until the dough comes together. Knead it for about 5-7 minutes until it's smooth and elastic. If it's too sticky, you can add a bit more flour.
4. Place the dough in a lightly greased bowl, cover it with a kitchen towel, and let it rise for about 1 hour, or until it's doubled in size.

Preparing the Filling:

1. In a skillet, melt the butter over medium heat. Add the chopped bacon and onions. Sauté until the bacon is crisp, and the onions are soft and translucent.
2. Season the filling with salt and pepper to taste. Remove from heat and let it cool.

Assembling the Pīrāgi:

1. Preheat your oven to 200°C (400°F).

2. Punch down the risen dough and roll it out on a floured surface into a large rectangle, about 1/4 inch thick.
3. Cut the dough into squares, about 3-4 inches in size.
4. Place a spoonful of the bacon and onion filling in the center of each square.
5. Fold the dough over the filling to create a triangle and pinch the edges to seal.
6. Place the filled buns on a baking sheet lined with parchment paper.
7. Brush the tops of the buns with the beaten egg.

Baking:

1. Bake the Pīrāgi in the preheated oven for about 15-20 minutes, or until they're golden brown.
2. Remove them from the oven and let them cool slightly before serving.

SVĒTKU MAIZE (RYE BREAD FOR FESTIVALS)

Servings: 1 loaf **Time:** 24-48 hours (including rising and resting time)

Ingredients:

For the Rye Bread Starter (Rye Sour):

- 1/2 cup rye flour
- 1/2 cup water
- 1/4 teaspoon active dry yeast (optional)

For the Rye Bread Dough:

- Rye sour (starter) from above
- 1 1/2 cups rye flour
- 1 1/2 cups all-purpose flour
- 1 1/2 teaspoons salt
- 1 1/2 cups lukewarm water
- 2 tablespoons molasses or honey
- 1/4 cup vegetable oil

Instructions:

Preparing the Rye Bread Starter (Rye Sour):

1. In a mixing bowl, combine the rye flour and water. If you want to speed up the fermentation process, you can add 1/4 teaspoon of active dry yeast to the mixture. Mix well to form a thick paste.
2. Cover the bowl with a clean kitchen towel and let it sit at room temperature for 12-24 hours, or until it becomes bubbly and fermented.

Mixing the Rye Bread Dough:

1. In a large mixing bowl, combine the rye sour (starter) from the previous step with rye flour, all-purpose flour, and salt.
2. In a separate bowl, mix together lukewarm water, molasses or honey, and vegetable oil.
3. Add the wet mixture to the dry mixture and stir until a sticky dough forms.
4. Knead the dough on a floured surface for about 10-15 minutes, or until it becomes smooth and elastic. Add more flour if needed to prevent sticking.

Rising and Shaping:

1. Place the dough in a greased bowl, cover it with a kitchen towel, and let it rise at room temperature for 4-6 hours or until it has doubled in size.
2. Once the dough has risen, shape it into a round or oval loaf and place it on a baking sheet lined with parchment paper.
3. Cover the loaf with a clean kitchen towel and let it rest for an additional 2-4 hours.

Baking:

1. Preheat your oven to 220°C (430°F).
2. Score the top of the bread with a sharp knife or blade to allow for even rising during baking.
3. Bake the Svētku maize in the preheated oven for about 35-40 minutes, or until it has a deep brown crust and sounds hollow when tapped on the bottom.
4. Let the bread cool on a wire rack before slicing and serving.

VEGETARIAN AND VEGAN DISHES

SĒŅU BIEŠU ZUPA (MUSHROOM BEET SOUP)

Servings: 4-6 **Time:** 1 hour

Ingredients:

- 2 cups fresh or canned beets, peeled and diced
- 200g (7 oz) fresh mushrooms, sliced
- 1 onion, finely chopped
- 2 cloves garlic, minced
- 2 tablespoons vegetable oil
- 4 cups vegetable broth
- 2 large potatoes, peeled and diced
- 1 carrot, peeled and diced
- 2 bay leaves

- 1 teaspoon dried dill or 1-2 sprigs fresh dill
- Salt and pepper to taste
- Sour cream or vegan sour cream for garnish (optional)

Instructions:

1. Sauté the Vegetables:

- In a large pot, heat the vegetable oil over medium heat. Add the finely chopped onion and minced garlic. Sauté until they become soft and translucent.
- Add the sliced mushrooms and continue to cook for another 5-7 minutes, or until the mushrooms release their moisture and start to brown.

2. Add Beets, Potatoes, and Carrots:

- Stir in the diced beets, potatoes, and carrots.
- Pour in the vegetable broth to cover the vegetables. Add the bay leaves and dried dill (if using). Season with salt and pepper to taste.

3. Simmer:

- Bring the soup to a boil, then reduce the heat to low and let it simmer for about 30-40 minutes, or until the beets, potatoes, and carrots are tender.

4. Serve:

- Remove the bay leaves and fresh dill sprigs (if using).
- Ladle the Sēņu biešu zupa into bowls.

- Optionally, garnish with a dollop of sour cream or vegan sour cream, and sprinkle with fresh dill if desired.

SIERPUTRA (COTTAGE CHEESE PORRIDGE)

Servings: 4-6 **Time:** 30 minutes

Ingredients:

- 1 cup semolina (cream of wheat)
- 4 cups milk
- 1 cup cottage cheese (curd cheese), finely crumbled
- 1/4 cup unsalted butter
- 1/4 cup granulated sugar (adjust to taste)
- 1/2 teaspoon vanilla extract
- A pinch of salt
- Fresh berries or fruit preserves for topping (optional)

Instructions:

1. Cook Semolina:

- In a medium-sized pot, bring the milk to a simmer over medium heat. Stir in the semolina.
- Cook, stirring constantly, until the mixture thickens and becomes smooth. This should take about 5-7 minutes.

2. Add Cottage Cheese:

- Reduce the heat to low, and stir in the crumbled cottage cheese (curd cheese). Continue to cook, stirring, for an additional 2-3 minutes until the cottage cheese softens and integrates with the semolina.

3. Sweeten and Flavor:

- Stir in the unsalted butter, granulated sugar, vanilla extract, and a pinch of salt. Adjust the sugar to your desired level of sweetness.
- Cook for an additional 2-3 minutes, ensuring all the ingredients are well combined.

4. Serve:

- Remove the pot from heat.
- Serve the Sierputra in bowls while it's still warm. You can top it with fresh berries or a dollop of fruit preserves for extra flavor.

VEGETĀRAIS PĪRĀGS (VEGETABLE PIE)

Servings: 6-8 **Time:** 1 hour

Ingredients:

For the Pie Crust:

- 2 cups all-purpose flour
- 1/2 cup cold unsalted butter, cubed
- 1/2 cup cold water
- 1/2 teaspoon salt

For the Filling:

- 2 cups mixed vegetables (e.g., peas, carrots, corn, beans), fresh or frozen
- 1 medium onion, finely chopped
- 1 red bell pepper, diced
- 2 cloves garlic, minced
- 2 tablespoons vegetable oil
- 1 cup grated cheese (e.g., cheddar or mozzarella)
- 1 teaspoon dried thyme
- Salt and pepper to taste
- 1 egg, beaten (for egg wash)

Instructions:

Preparing the Pie Crust:

1. In a large mixing bowl, combine the all-purpose flour and salt.
2. Add the cold, cubed butter to the flour mixture. Use a pastry cutter or your fingers to cut the butter into the flour until the mixture resembles coarse crumbs.
3. Gradually add cold water, one tablespoon at a time, and mix until the dough comes together. Be careful not to overwork the dough.
4. Shape the dough into a disk, wrap it in plastic wrap, and refrigerate for at least 30 minutes.

Preparing the Filling:

1. In a large skillet, heat the vegetable oil over medium heat.
2. Add the finely chopped onion and minced garlic. Sauté until they become soft and translucent.

3. Add the diced red bell pepper and mixed vegetables. Cook for about 5-7 minutes, or until they become tender.
4. Stir in the dried thyme, salt, and pepper to taste.
5. Remove the skillet from heat and let the vegetable mixture cool.

Assembling the Pie:

1. Preheat your oven to 190°C (375°F).
2. On a floured surface, roll out the chilled dough into a circle large enough to line a 9-inch pie dish.
3. Carefully transfer the rolled-out dough to the pie dish, pressing it down to fit and trimming any excess.
4. Spread half of the grated cheese over the bottom of the pie crust.
5. Add the cooled vegetable mixture on top of the cheese.
6. Sprinkle the remaining cheese over the vegetables.

Baking:

1. Place the pie in the preheated oven and bake for about 30-35 minutes, or until the crust is golden and the filling is hot and bubbly.
2. About halfway through baking, brush the top of the pie with the beaten egg for a golden finish.
3. Remove the pie from the oven and let it cool for a few minutes before slicing and serving.

BIEZPIENA PLĀCENĪŠI (COTTAGE CHEESE PANCAKES)

Servings: 4-6 **Time:** 30 minutes

Ingredients:

- 500g (about 1 lb) cottage cheese (curd cheese)
- 2 large eggs
- 3-4 tablespoons granulated sugar (adjust to taste)
- 1 teaspoon vanilla extract
- Zest of 1 lemon (optional)
- 1/2 cup all-purpose flour
- 1/2 teaspoon baking powder
- Pinch of salt
- Vegetable oil, for frying
- Sour cream or jam, for serving (optional)

Instructions:

1. Prepare the Batter:

- In a mixing bowl, combine the cottage cheese, eggs, granulated sugar, vanilla extract, and lemon zest (if using). Mix until the ingredients are well combined.
- In a separate bowl, whisk together the all-purpose flour, baking powder, and a pinch of salt.
- Gradually add the dry ingredients to the cottage cheese mixture, stirring until you have a smooth batter.

2. Heat the Griddle or Pan:

- Heat a griddle or a large skillet over medium heat and lightly grease it with vegetable oil.

3. Cook the Pancakes:

- Drop spoonfuls of the batter onto the hot griddle to form pancakes. You can make them as small or as large as you prefer.
- Cook until the pancakes begin to set and small bubbles form on the surface, usually about 2-3 minutes.
- Flip the pancakes and cook the other side until they are golden brown and cooked through, about 2-3 minutes more.

4. Serve:

- Remove the Biezpiena plācenīši from the griddle and place them on a plate lined with paper towels to absorb any excess oil.
- Serve the cottage cheese pancakes hot, with a dollop of sour cream or a spoonful of jam, if desired.

VEGETABLE STIR-FRY

Servings: 4 **Time:** 20 minutes

Ingredients:

For the Stir-Fry Sauce:

- 3 tablespoons soy sauce
- 2 tablespoons hoisin sauce
- 1 tablespoon rice vinegar
- 1 teaspoon sugar
- 1/2 teaspoon ginger, minced
- 1/2 teaspoon garlic, minced

For the Stir-Fry:

- 2 tablespoons vegetable oil
- 1 onion, sliced
- 2 cloves garlic, minced
- 1 red bell pepper, sliced
- 1 yellow bell pepper, sliced
- 1 cup broccoli florets
- 1 cup snap peas, ends trimmed
- 1 carrot, julienned
- 1 zucchini, sliced
- 1 cup mushrooms, sliced
- Salt and pepper to taste
- Cooked rice or noodles, for serving

Instructions:

1. Prepare the Stir-Fry Sauce:

- In a small bowl, whisk together the soy sauce, hoisin sauce, rice vinegar, sugar, minced ginger, and minced garlic. Set the sauce aside.

2. Sauté the Vegetables:

- Heat the vegetable oil in a large skillet or wok over high heat.
- Add the sliced onion and minced garlic, and stir-fry for about 1-2 minutes until they become fragrant and slightly softened.
- Add the bell peppers, broccoli, snap peas, carrot, zucchini, and mushrooms to the skillet. Stir-fry for about 4-5 minutes, or until the vegetables are tender-crisp.

3. Add the Sauce:

- Pour the stir-fry sauce over the cooked vegetables. Stir well to coat all the vegetables with the sauce.
- Season with salt and pepper to taste. Stir-fry for an additional 1-2 minutes to heat the sauce and let it thicken slightly.

4. Serve:

- Serve the vegetable stir-fry over cooked rice or noodles

TIME-HONORED FAVORITES

KARTUPEĻU PANKŪKAS (POTATO PANCAKES)

Servings: 4 **Time:** 30 minutes

Ingredients:

- 4 large russet potatoes, peeled
- 1 small onion, finely grated
- 2 eggs, beaten
- 2 tablespoons all-purpose flour
- 1/2 teaspoon salt
- 1/4 teaspoon black pepper
- Vegetable oil, for frying
- Sour cream or applesauce, for serving (optional)

Instructions:

1. Prepare the Potatoes:

- Grate the peeled potatoes using the fine side of a box grater or a food processor.
- Place the grated potatoes in a clean kitchen towel and squeeze out as much liquid as possible.

2. Combine the Ingredients:

- In a large mixing bowl, combine the grated potatoes, finely grated onion, beaten eggs, all-purpose flour, salt, and black pepper. Mix well until all ingredients are fully incorporated.

3. Heat the Oil:

- In a large skillet, heat about 1/4 inch of vegetable oil over medium-high heat. The oil should be hot but not smoking.

4. Fry the Pancakes:

- Using a spoon or your hands, carefully drop spoonfuls of the potato mixture into the hot oil. Flatten each spoonful with a spatula to form a pancake.
- Fry the pancakes until they are golden brown and crispy on both sides, about 3-4 minutes per side. You may need to adjust the heat to prevent burning.
- Place the cooked pancakes on a plate lined with paper towels to drain any excess oil.

5. Serve:

- Serve the Kartupeļu pankūkas hot, with a dollop of sour cream or applesauce if desired.

KARBONĀDE (PORK SCHNITZEL)

Servings: 4 **Time:** 30 minutes

Ingredients:

- 4 boneless pork chops, about 1/2 inch thick
- Salt and pepper, to taste
- 1 cup all-purpose flour
- 2 large eggs
- 1 cup breadcrumbs (preferably panko)
- Vegetable oil, for frying
- Lemon wedges, for serving (optional)

Instructions:

1. Prepare the Pork Chops:

- Place the boneless pork chops between two sheets of plastic wrap or parchment paper.
- Use a meat mallet or rolling pin to gently pound the pork chops until they are about 1/4 inch thick.
- Season both sides of the pork chops with salt and pepper.

2. Set Up a Breading Station:

- In three separate shallow dishes, set up a breading station. Place the flour in the first dish, beat the eggs in the second dish, and put the breadcrumbs in the third dish.

3. Bread the Pork Chops:

- Dredge each pork chop in the flour, making sure to coat it evenly. Shake off any excess flour.
- Dip the floured pork chop into the beaten eggs, allowing any excess to drip off.
- Press the pork chop into the breadcrumbs, coating it thoroughly. Press the breadcrumbs onto the meat to adhere.

4. Fry the Schnitzel:

- In a large skillet, heat about 1/4 inch of vegetable oil over medium-high heat.
- Once the oil is hot, carefully add the breaded pork chops to the skillet. Cook for about 3-4 minutes per side, or until they are golden brown and the pork is cooked through.
- Place the cooked schnitzel on a plate lined with paper towels to drain any excess oil.

5. Serve:

- Serve the Karbonāde hot, with lemon wedges if desired.

ĶOŅI (CABBAGE AND PORK STEW)

Servings: 4-6 **Time:** 2 hours

Ingredients:

- 1 lb pork shoulder, cubed
- 1 large head of cabbage, finely shredded
- 1 large onion, chopped
- 2 carrots, peeled and diced
- 2 cloves garlic, minced
- 2 tablespoons vegetable oil
- 1 cup water or broth
- 2 bay leaves
- Salt and pepper, to taste
- Sour cream, for serving (optional)

Instructions:

1. Brown the Pork:

- In a large pot or Dutch oven, heat the vegetable oil over medium-high heat.
- Add the cubed pork and brown it on all sides. This should take about 5-7 minutes.

2. Sauté the Vegetables:

- Add the chopped onion and diced carrots to the pot. Sauté for about 5 minutes, or until the vegetables start to soften.
- Stir in the minced garlic and continue to cook for another minute, until fragrant.

3. Add the Cabbage:

- Add the finely shredded cabbage to the pot. Stir well to combine the cabbage with the other ingredients.
- Cook for a few minutes until the cabbage starts to wilt and reduce in volume.

4. Simmer:

- Pour in the water or broth and add the bay leaves.
- Season with salt and pepper to taste.
- Bring the mixture to a simmer. Reduce the heat to low, cover the pot, and let it simmer for about 1 to 1.5 hours, or until the pork is tender, and the flavors meld together.

5. Serve:

- Remove the bay leaves.
- Serve Ķoņi hot, with a dollop of sour cream if desired.

MELNIE ZIRŅI AR SPEĶI (BLACK PEAS WITH BACON)

Servings: 4-6 **Time:** 1.5 hours (plus soaking time)

Ingredients:

- 1 cup black peas (black-eyed peas or black beans)
- 200g (about 7 oz) smoked bacon, chopped
- 1 large onion, finely chopped
- 2 cloves garlic, minced
- 1 bay leaf
- 1 teaspoon dried marjoram
- 1/2 teaspoon salt (or to taste)

- 1/4 teaspoon black pepper
- 6 cups water
- Fresh parsley, for garnish (optional)

Instructions:

1. Soak the Black Peas:

- In a large bowl, soak the black peas in cold water for at least 6 hours or overnight. Drain and rinse before using.

2. Cook the Bacon:

- In a large pot, over medium heat, cook the chopped smoked bacon until it becomes crispy and releases its fat, about 5-7 minutes.

3. Sauté Onions and Garlic:

- Add the finely chopped onion to the bacon and cook until it becomes soft and translucent, about 3-5 minutes.
- Stir in the minced garlic and cook for an additional minute until fragrant.

4. Add Black Peas:

- Add the soaked and drained black peas to the pot.
- Pour in 6 cups of water.
- Add the bay leaf, dried marjoram, salt, and black pepper.

5. Simmer:

- Bring the mixture to a boil, then reduce the heat to low. Cover the pot and let the peas simmer for about 1 to 1.5 hours, or until the peas are tender. The cooking time may vary depending on the age of the peas, so be sure to taste and test for doneness.

6. Serve:

- Remove the bay leaf.
- Serve Melnie zirņi ar speķi hot, garnished with fresh parsley if desired.

RAUGI (DILL-PICKLED CUCUMBERS)

Servings: Varies (depends on the number of cucumbers)
Time: 30 minutes (plus pickling time)

Ingredients:

- Cucumbers (as many as you'd like to pickle)
- Fresh dill fronds
- 2-3 cloves of garlic, peeled and lightly crushed
- 1-2 dried red chili peppers (optional, for some heat)
- 1-2 bay leaves
- 1 tablespoon whole black peppercorns
- 1 tablespoon whole coriander seeds
- 1 tablespoon coarse salt
- Water
- Vinegar (white or apple cider vinegar)

Instructions:

1. Prepare the Cucumbers:

- Wash the cucumbers thoroughly and trim off both ends.
- If the cucumbers are large, you can slice them into spears or thick coins if you prefer.

2. Pack the Jars:

- Sterilize glass jars with lids, and let them cool.
- Begin by placing a layer of fresh dill fronds in the bottom of each jar.
- Add the peeled and lightly crushed garlic cloves, dried red chili peppers (if using), bay leaves, black peppercorns, and coriander seeds to the jars.
- Carefully pack the cucumbers into the jars, making sure they are snug but not too tightly packed.

3. Prepare the Brine:

- In a separate pot, mix 1 liter of water with 1 cup of vinegar and 1 tablespoon of coarse salt. Adjust the amount depending on the number of cucumbers you have. You'll need enough brine to cover the cucumbers in the jars.

4. Fill the Jars with Brine:

- Pour the brine into each jar, ensuring that the cucumbers are completely submerged. Leave a little headspace at the top of each jar.

5. Seal the Jars:

- Place the lids on the jars and close them tightly.

6. Store and Wait:

- Let the jars sit at room temperature for 1-2 days to allow the pickling process to begin.
- After the initial waiting period, store the jars in the refrigerator for several days to several weeks for the flavors to fully develop. The longer they sit, the more intense the flavor will become.
- You can start tasting the pickles after a few days to determine the level of sourness you prefer. Once they've reached the desired taste, they are ready to be enjoyed.

SPECIAL OCCASION CAKES

MIERĪGĀ TORTE (PEACE CAKE)

Servings: 10-12 **Time:** 2 hours

Ingredients:

For the Cake Layers:

- 2 cups all-purpose flour
- 2 teaspoons baking powder
- 1/2 teaspoon salt
- 1/2 cup unsalted butter, at room temperature
- 1 cup granulated sugar
- 4 large eggs
- 1 teaspoon vanilla extract
- 1/2 cup whole milk

For the Filling and Frosting:

- 2 cups sour cream
- 1 cup heavy cream
- 1 cup powdered sugar
- 1 teaspoon vanilla extract

For Garnish:

- Fresh berries (strawberries, blueberries, or raspberries)
- Mint leaves
- Powdered sugar for dusting

Instructions:

1. Prepare the Cake Layers:

- Preheat your oven to 350°F (175°C). Grease and line two 9-inch round cake pans with parchment paper.
- In a medium bowl, whisk together the all-purpose flour, baking powder, and salt. Set aside.
- In a large mixing bowl, beat the unsalted butter and granulated sugar together until light and fluffy, about 2-3 minutes.
- Add the eggs one at a time, beating well after each addition. Stir in the vanilla extract.
- Gradually add the dry ingredients to the wet ingredients, alternating with the whole milk, beginning and ending with the dry ingredients. Mix until just combined.
- Divide the cake batter evenly between the prepared cake pans and smooth the tops.

- Bake in the preheated oven for 25-30 minutes, or until a toothpick inserted into the center comes out clean.
- Remove the cakes from the oven and let them cool in the pans for 10 minutes. Then, transfer the cake layers to a wire rack to cool completely.

2. Prepare the Filling and Frosting:

- In a mixing bowl, combine the sour cream, heavy cream, powdered sugar, and vanilla extract. Beat until the mixture is smooth and well combined.

3. Assemble the Cake:

- Place one of the cooled cake layers on a serving plate.
- Spread a generous layer of the sour cream and cream mixture over the top of the first layer.
- Place the second cake layer on top and press down gently.
- Use the remaining cream mixture to frost the top and sides of the cake. Smooth the frosting with a spatula.

4. Garnish:

- Decorate the cake with fresh berries and mint leaves.
- Dust the top of the cake with powdered sugar.

5. Chill and Serve:

- Refrigerate the Mierīgā torte for at least 2 hours before serving to allow the flavors to meld.

LĀČPLĒŠA DIENAS KŪKA
(INDEPENDENCE DAY CAKE)

Servings: 8-10 **Time:** 2 hours

Ingredients:

For the Cake:

- 2 cups all-purpose flour
- 2 teaspoons baking powder
- 1/2 teaspoon salt
- 1/2 cup unsalted butter, at room temperature
- 1 cup granulated sugar
- 4 large eggs
- 1 teaspoon vanilla extract
- 1/2 cup whole milk

For the Filling:

- 2 cups fresh or frozen mixed berries (strawberries, blueberries, raspberries, etc.)
- 1/2 cup granulated sugar
- 2 tablespoons cornstarch

For the Frosting:

- 2 cups heavy cream
- 1/4 cup powdered sugar
- 1 teaspoon vanilla extract

For Garnish:

- Fresh berries

- Edible flowers (optional)
- Powdered sugar for dusting

Instructions:

1. Prepare the Cake:

- Preheat your oven to 350°F (175°C). Grease and line two 9-inch round cake pans with parchment paper.
- In a medium bowl, whisk together the all-purpose flour, baking powder, and salt. Set aside.
- In a large mixing bowl, beat the unsalted butter and granulated sugar together until light and fluffy, about 2-3 minutes.
- Add the eggs one at a time, beating well after each addition. Stir in the vanilla extract.
- Gradually add the dry ingredients to the wet ingredients, alternating with the whole milk, beginning and ending with the dry ingredients. Mix until just combined.
- Divide the cake batter evenly between the prepared cake pans and smooth the tops.
- Bake in the preheated oven for 25-30 minutes, or until a toothpick inserted into the center comes out clean.
- Remove the cakes from the oven and let them cool in the pans for 10 minutes. Then, transfer the cake layers to a wire rack to cool completely.

2. Prepare the Filling:

- In a saucepan, combine the mixed berries, granulated sugar, and cornstarch. Cook over medium heat, stirring constantly, until the mixture thickens and the berries break down, about 5-7 minutes. Remove from heat and let it cool.

3. Prepare the Frosting:

- In a mixing bowl, whip the heavy cream until it starts to thicken. Add the powdered sugar and vanilla extract and continue whipping until it reaches stiff peaks.

4. Assemble the Cake:

- Place one of the cooled cake layers on a serving plate.
- Spread a generous layer of the berry filling over the top of the first layer.
- Place the second cake layer on top and press down gently.
- Use the whipped cream frosting to frost the top and sides of the cake. You can create decorative patterns with a spatula.

5. Garnish:

- Decorate the cake with fresh berries and edible flowers if desired.
- Dust the top of the cake with powdered sugar.

6. Chill and Serve:

- Refrigerate the Lāčplēša dienas kūka for at least 2 hours before serving to allow the flavors to meld.

BUMBIERU TORTE (PEAR CAKE)

Servings: 8-10 **Time:** 1.5 hours

Ingredients:

For the Cake:

- 2 cups all-purpose flour
- 1 1/2 teaspoons baking powder
- 1/2 teaspoon salt
- 1/2 cup unsalted butter, at room temperature
- 1 cup granulated sugar
- 3 large eggs
- 1 teaspoon vanilla extract
- 1/2 cup whole milk

For the Pear Filling:

- 4 ripe pears, peeled, cored, and sliced
- 1/4 cup granulated sugar
- 1 teaspoon ground cinnamon

For the Streusel Topping:

- 1/2 cup all-purpose flour
- 1/2 cup granulated sugar
- 1/4 cup unsalted butter, cold and cubed

For Garnish:

- Powdered sugar for dusting
- Whipped cream (optional)

Instructions:

1. Prepare the Cake:

- Preheat your oven to 350°F (175°C). Grease and line a 9-inch round cake pan with parchment paper.
- In a medium bowl, whisk together the all-purpose flour, baking powder, and salt. Set aside.
- In a large mixing bowl, beat the unsalted butter and granulated sugar together until light and fluffy, about 2-3 minutes.
- Add the eggs one at a time, beating well after each addition. Stir in the vanilla extract.
- Gradually add the dry ingredients to the wet ingredients, alternating with the whole milk, beginning and ending with the dry ingredients. Mix until just combined.

2. Prepare the Pear Filling:

- In a separate bowl, toss the sliced pears with the granulated sugar and ground cinnamon.

3. Make the Streusel Topping:

- In a small bowl, combine the all-purpose flour and granulated sugar. Cut in the cold, cubed unsalted butter until the mixture forms crumbly streusel.

4. Assemble the Cake:

- Spread half of the cake batter in the prepared cake pan.
- Layer the pear slices over the cake batter.
- Drop spoonfuls of the remaining cake batter over the pears.

- Sprinkle the streusel topping evenly over the top of the cake.

5. Bake:

- Bake in the preheated oven for 45-50 minutes, or until the cake is golden brown and a toothpick inserted into the center comes out clean.

6. Cool and Garnish:

- Let the cake cool in the pan for about 10 minutes before transferring it to a wire rack to cool completely.
- Dust the top of the Bumbieru torte with powdered sugar before serving.
- You can serve this cake with a dollop of whipped cream if desired.

MEDUS KŪKA (HONEY CAKE)

Servings: 10-12 **Time:** 3-4 hours (including chilling time)

Ingredients:

For the Cake Layers:

- 2 cups all-purpose flour
- 1 teaspoon baking soda
- 1 teaspoon ground cinnamon
- 1/2 teaspoon ground ginger
- 1/2 teaspoon ground cloves
- 1/4 teaspoon salt

- 1/2 cup unsalted butter, at room temperature
- 1 cup granulated sugar
- 4 large eggs
- 2 tablespoons honey
- 1 teaspoon vanilla extract

For the Filling and Frosting:

- 2 cups heavy cream
- 1 cup powdered sugar
- 2 tablespoons honey
- 1 teaspoon vanilla extract

For Garnish:

- Chopped nuts (walnuts or hazelnuts), optional
- Chocolate shavings, optional

Instructions:

1. Prepare the Cake Layers:

- Preheat your oven to 350°F (175°C). Grease and line two 9-inch round cake pans with parchment paper.
- In a medium bowl, whisk together the all-purpose flour, baking soda, ground cinnamon, ground ginger, ground cloves, and salt. Set aside.
- In a large mixing bowl, beat the unsalted butter and granulated sugar together until light and fluffy, about 2-3 minutes.
- Add the eggs one at a time, beating well after each addition. Stir in the honey and vanilla extract.
- Gradually add the dry ingredients to the wet ingredients, mixing until just combined.

- Divide the cake batter evenly between the prepared cake pans and smooth the tops.
- Bake in the preheated oven for 25-30 minutes, or until a toothpick inserted into the center comes out clean.
- Remove the cakes from the oven and let them cool in the pans for 10 minutes. Then, transfer the cake layers to a wire rack to cool completely.

2. Prepare the Filling and Frosting:

- In a mixing bowl, whip the heavy cream until it begins to thicken.
- Add the powdered sugar, honey, and vanilla extract, and continue whipping until it reaches stiff peaks.

3. Assemble the Cake:

- Place one of the cooled cake layers on a serving plate.
- Spread a generous layer of the whipped cream filling over the top of the first layer.
- Place the second cake layer on top and press down gently.
- Use the remaining whipped cream frosting to frost the top and sides of the cake. You can create decorative patterns with a spatula.

4. Garnish:

- Optionally, you can garnish the cake with chopped nuts and chocolate shavings.

5. Chill and Serve:

- Refrigerate the Medus kūka for at least 2 hours before serving to allow the flavors to meld.

SARKANĀSKU TORTE (RED CURRANT CAKE)

Servings: 8-10 **Time:** 1.5 hours

Ingredients:

For the Cake:

- 1 1/2 cups all-purpose flour
- 1 1/2 teaspoons baking powder
- 1/2 teaspoon salt
- 1/2 cup unsalted butter, at room temperature
- 1 cup granulated sugar
- 3 large eggs
- 1 teaspoon vanilla extract
- 1/2 cup whole milk

For the Red Currant Filling:

- 2 cups fresh red currants, stems removed
- 1/2 cup granulated sugar

For the Frosting:

- 2 cups heavy cream
- 1/4 cup powdered sugar
- 1 teaspoon vanilla extract

For Garnish:

- Additional red currants
- Fresh mint leaves (optional)

Instructions:

1. Prepare the Cake:

- Preheat your oven to 350°F (175°C). Grease and line a 9-inch round cake pan with parchment paper.
- In a medium bowl, whisk together the all-purpose flour, baking powder, and salt. Set aside.
- In a large mixing bowl, beat the unsalted butter and granulated sugar together until light and fluffy, about 2-3 minutes.
- Add the eggs one at a time, beating well after each addition. Stir in the vanilla extract.
- Gradually add the dry ingredients to the wet ingredients, alternating with the whole milk, beginning and ending with the dry ingredients. Mix until just combined.
- Pour the cake batter into the prepared cake pan.

2. Prepare the Red Currant Filling:

- In a separate bowl, mix the fresh red currants and granulated sugar. Set aside to macerate for about 10 minutes.
- After macerating, gently spoon the red currant mixture over the cake batter in the pan. The currants will sink into the batter as the cake bakes.

3. Bake:

- Bake in the preheated oven for 35-40 minutes, or until a toothpick inserted into the center of the cake comes out clean.

4. Cool:

- Remove the cake from the oven and let it cool in the pan for 10 minutes before transferring it to a wire rack to cool completely.

5. Prepare the Frosting:

- In a mixing bowl, whip the heavy cream until it begins to thicken.
- Add the powdered sugar and vanilla extract, and continue whipping until it reaches stiff peaks.

6. Frost and Garnish:

- Once the cake is completely cooled, spread a generous layer of the whipped cream frosting over the top of the cake.
- Optionally, garnish with additional red currants and fresh mint leaves.

7. Chill and Serve:

- Refrigerate the Sarkanāsku torte for at least 2 hours before serving to allow the flavors to meld.

PIES AND TARTS

ĀBOLU PĪRĀGS (APPLE PIE)

Servings: 8-10 Time: 1.5 hours

Ingredients:

For the Crust:

- 2 1/2 cups all-purpose flour
- 1 teaspoon salt
- 1 cup unsalted butter, cold and cubed
- 6-8 tablespoons ice-cold water

For the Apple Filling:

- 6-7 medium-sized apples (tart variety, such as Granny Smith), peeled, cored, and sliced
- 1/2 cup granulated sugar
- 1 teaspoon ground cinnamon
- 1/4 teaspoon ground nutmeg (optional)
- 1 tablespoon lemon juice

For the Topping:

- 1/2 cup all-purpose flour
- 1/2 cup granulated sugar
- 1/2 cup unsalted butter, at room temperature
- 1/2 cup rolled oats

Instructions:

1. Prepare the Crust:

- In a large bowl, combine the all-purpose flour and salt.
- Add the cold, cubed unsalted butter to the flour mixture. Using a pastry cutter or your fingers, work the butter into the flour until the mixture resembles coarse crumbs.
- Gradually add the ice-cold water, one tablespoon at a time, and mix until the dough comes together. Be careful not to overmix.
- Divide the dough in half and shape each half into a disk. Wrap them in plastic wrap and refrigerate for at least 30 minutes.

2. Prepare the Apple Filling:

- In a large bowl, combine the sliced apples, granulated sugar, ground cinnamon, ground nutmeg (if using), and lemon juice. Toss to coat the apples evenly and set aside.

3. Preheat the Oven:

- Preheat your oven to 375°F (190°C).

4. Roll Out the Crust:

- Take one of the chilled dough disks and roll it out on a floured surface to fit a 9-inch pie dish. Transfer the rolled-out dough to the pie dish.

5. Assemble the Pie:

- Arrange the prepared apple filling in the pie dish with the rolled-out crust.

6. Prepare the Topping:

- In a separate bowl, combine the all-purpose flour, granulated sugar, unsalted butter, and rolled oats. Mix until you have a crumbly streusel-like topping.

7. Add the Topping:

- Sprinkle the streusel topping evenly over the apples in the pie dish.

8. Roll Out the Second Crust:

- Roll out the second chilled dough disk on a floured surface.
- You can use it to cover the pie completely or create a lattice or decorative pattern as desired.

9. Bake:

- Place the pie in the preheated oven and bake for 45-55 minutes, or until the crust is golden brown and the apple filling is bubbly.

10. Cool and Serve:

- Allow the Ābolu pīrāgs to cool for a bit before serving. It's delicious on its own or with a scoop of vanilla ice cream.

RIEKSTU PĪRĀGS (NUT TART)

Servings: 8-10 Time: 1.5 hours

Ingredients:

For the Crust:

- 1 1/4 cups all-purpose flour
- 1/4 cup granulated sugar
- 1/4 teaspoon salt
- 1/2 cup unsalted butter, cold and cubed
- 1 large egg yolk
- 2-3 tablespoons ice-cold water

For the Nut Filling:

- 2 cups mixed nuts (walnuts, hazelnuts, or pecans), finely chopped
- 1 cup granulated sugar
- 1/2 cup unsalted butter, melted
- 1/4 cup heavy cream
- 2 large eggs
- 1 teaspoon vanilla extract

Instructions:

1. Prepare the Crust:

    - In a food processor, combine the all-purpose flour, granulated sugar, and salt. Pulse to mix.
    - Add the cold, cubed unsalted butter and pulse until the mixture resembles coarse crumbs.
    - In a small bowl, whisk the egg yolk with 2 tablespoons of ice-cold water.
    - While the food processor is running, pour the egg yolk mixture through the feed tube. Continue processing until the dough comes together. If the dough is too dry, add an additional tablespoon of ice-cold water.
    - Turn the dough out onto a floured surface, shape it into a disk, and wrap it in plastic wrap. Refrigerate for at least 30 minutes.

2. Preheat the Oven:

    - Preheat your oven to 350°F (175°C).

3. Roll Out the Crust:

- On a floured surface, roll out the chilled dough to fit a 9-inch tart pan. Transfer the rolled-out dough to the tart pan and trim any excess.

4. Prepare the Nut Filling:

- In a mixing bowl, combine the finely chopped mixed nuts, granulated sugar, melted unsalted butter, heavy cream, eggs, and vanilla extract. Mix until well combined.

5. Assemble the Tart:

- Pour the nut filling into the prepared tart crust.

6. Bake:

- Place the tart in the preheated oven and bake for 30-35 minutes, or until the filling is set and the crust is golden brown.

7. Cool and Serve:

- Allow the Riekstu pīrāgs to cool in the tart pan before removing it. You can serve it at room temperature.

ĶIRBJU PĪRĀGS (PUMPKIN PIE)

Servings: 8-10 Time: 2 hours

Ingredients:

For the Pie Crust:

- 1 1/4 cups all-purpose flour
- 1/2 teaspoon salt
- 1/2 cup unsalted butter, cold and cubed
- 4-5 tablespoons ice-cold water

For the Pumpkin Filling:

- 2 cups pumpkin puree (canned or homemade)
- 1/2 cup granulated sugar
- 1/4 cup brown sugar
- 1 teaspoon ground cinnamon
- 1/2 teaspoon ground ginger
- 1/4 teaspoon ground nutmeg
- 1/4 teaspoon ground cloves
- 1/4 teaspoon salt
- 2 large eggs
- 1 cup heavy cream
- 1 teaspoon vanilla extract

Instructions:

1. Prepare the Pie Crust:

- In a food processor, combine the all-purpose flour and salt. Pulse to mix.
- Add the cold, cubed unsalted butter and pulse until the mixture resembles coarse crumbs.
- While the food processor is running, pour 4 tablespoons of ice-cold water through the feed tube. Continue processing until the dough comes together. If the dough is too dry, add an additional tablespoon of ice-cold water.

- Turn the dough out onto a floured surface, shape it into a disk, and wrap it in plastic wrap. Refrigerate for at least 30 minutes.

2. Preheat the Oven:

- Preheat your oven to 425°F (220°C).

3. Roll Out the Pie Crust:

- On a floured surface, roll out the chilled dough to fit a 9-inch pie dish. Transfer the rolled-out dough to the pie dish and trim any excess.

4. Prepare the Pumpkin Filling:

- In a large mixing bowl, combine the pumpkin puree, granulated sugar, brown sugar, ground cinnamon, ground ginger, ground nutmeg, ground cloves, and salt. Mix until well combined.
- In a separate bowl, whisk the eggs, heavy cream, and vanilla extract.
- Gradually add the egg mixture to the pumpkin mixture and mix until everything is fully combined.

5. Fill the Pie Crust:

- Pour the pumpkin filling into the prepared pie crust.

6. Bake:

- Place the pie in the preheated oven and bake at 425°F (220°C) for 15 minutes.

- After 15 minutes, reduce the oven temperature to 350°F (175°C) and continue baking for an additional 40-50 minutes, or until the filling is set and a toothpick inserted into the center comes out clean.

7. Cool and Serve:

- Allow the Ķirbju pīrāgs to cool completely before slicing and serving.

RABARBERU PĪRĀGS (RHUBARB PIE)

Servings: 8-10 Time: 1.5 hours

Ingredients:

For the Pie Crust:

- 1 1/4 cups all-purpose flour
- 1/2 teaspoon salt
- 1/2 cup unsalted butter, cold and cubed
- 4-5 tablespoons ice-cold water

For the Rhubarb Filling:

- 4 cups fresh rhubarb, chopped into 1/2-inch pieces
- 1 1/2 cups granulated sugar
- 1/4 cup all-purpose flour
- 1/2 teaspoon ground cinnamon
- 1/4 teaspoon salt
- 1 tablespoon lemon juice

Instructions:

1. **Prepare the Pie Crust:**

   - In a food processor, combine the all-purpose flour and salt. Pulse to mix.
   - Add the cold, cubed unsalted butter and pulse until the mixture resembles coarse crumbs.
   - While the food processor is running, pour 4 tablespoons of ice-cold water through the feed tube. Continue processing until the dough comes together. If the dough is too dry, add an additional tablespoon of ice-cold water.
   - Turn the dough out onto a floured surface, shape it into a disk, and wrap it in plastic wrap. Refrigerate for at least 30 minutes.

2. **Preheat the Oven:**

   - Preheat your oven to 425°F (220°C).

3. **Roll Out the Pie Crust:**

   - On a floured surface, roll out the chilled dough to fit a 9-inch pie dish. Transfer the rolled-out dough to the pie dish and trim any excess.

4. **Prepare the Rhubarb Filling:**

   - In a large mixing bowl, combine the chopped fresh rhubarb, granulated sugar, all-purpose flour, ground cinnamon, salt, and lemon juice. Toss to coat the rhubarb evenly.

5. **Fill the Pie Crust:**

- Pour the rhubarb filling into the prepared pie crust.

6. Bake:

- Place the pie in the preheated oven and bake at 425°F (220°C) for 15 minutes.
- After 15 minutes, reduce the oven temperature to 350°F (175°C) and continue baking for an additional 40-50 minutes, or until the rhubarb filling is set and the crust is golden brown.

7. Cool and Serve:

- Allow the Rabarberu pīrāgs to cool completely before slicing and serving.

ĶIMEŅMAIZES PĪRĀGS (CARAWAY SEED PIE)

Servings: 8-10 Time: 1.5 hours

Ingredients:

For the Pie Crust:

- 1 1/4 cups all-purpose flour
- 1/2 teaspoon salt
- 1/2 cup unsalted butter, cold and cubed
- 4-5 tablespoons ice-cold water

For the Caraway Seed Filling:

- 2 cups whole milk

- 1/2 cup granulated sugar
- 3 large eggs
- 2 tablespoons caraway seeds
- 1/4 cup all-purpose flour
- 1/4 teaspoon salt
- 1/4 cup unsalted butter, melted
- 1 teaspoon vanilla extract

Instructions:

1. Prepare the Pie Crust:

   - In a food processor, combine the all-purpose flour and salt. Pulse to mix.
   - Add the cold, cubed unsalted butter and pulse until the mixture resembles coarse crumbs.
   - While the food processor is running, pour 4 tablespoons of ice-cold water through the feed tube. Continue processing until the dough comes together. If the dough is too dry, add an additional tablespoon of ice-cold water.
   - Turn the dough out onto a floured surface, shape it into a disk, and wrap it in plastic wrap. Refrigerate for at least 30 minutes.

2. Preheat the Oven:

   - Preheat your oven to 350°F (175°C).

3. Roll Out the Pie Crust:

- On a floured surface, roll out the chilled dough to fit a 9-inch pie dish. Transfer the rolled-out dough to the pie dish and trim any excess.

4. Prepare the Caraway Seed Filling:

- In a saucepan, heat the whole milk until it's just about to boil. Remove it from the heat and set it aside to cool slightly.
- In a mixing bowl, whisk together the granulated sugar and eggs until well combined.
- Slowly add the slightly cooled milk to the egg mixture, stirring constantly to avoid curdling. Mix in the caraway seeds, all-purpose flour, salt, melted unsalted butter, and vanilla extract. Ensure that the mixture is smooth and well combined.

5. Fill the Pie Crust:

- Pour the caraway seed filling into the prepared pie crust.

6. Bake:

- Place the pie in the preheated oven and bake at 350°F (175°C) for 40-45 minutes, or until the filling is set and the top is golden brown.

7. Cool and Serve:

- Allow the Ķimeņmaizes pīrāgs to cool completely before slicing and serving.

MEASUREMENT CONVERSIONS

Volume Conversions:

- 1 cup = 8 fluid ounces = 240 milliliters
- 1 tablespoon = 3 teaspoons = 15 milliliters
- 1 fluid ounce = 2 tablespoons = 30 milliliters
- 1 quart = 4 cups = 32 fluid ounces = 946 milliliters
- 1 gallon = 4 quarts = 128 fluid ounces = 3.78 liters
- 1 liter = 1,000 milliliters = 33.8 fluid ounces
- 1 milliliter = 0.034 fluid ounces = 0.002 cups

Weight Conversions:

- 1 pound = 16 ounces = 453.592 grams
- 1 ounce = 28.349 grams
- 1 gram = 0.035 ounces = 0.001 kilograms
- 1 kilogram = 1,000 grams = 35.274 ounces = 2.205 pounds

Temperature Conversions:

- To convert from Fahrenheit to Celsius: (°F - 32) / 1.8
- To convert from Celsius to Fahrenheit: (°C * 1.8) + 32

Length Conversions:

- 1 inch = 2.54 centimeters
- 1 foot = 12 inches = 30.48 centimeters
- 1 yard = 3 feet = 36 inches = 91.44 centimeters
- 1 meter = 100 centimeters = 1.094 yards
- 1 kilometer = 1,000 meters = 0.621 miles

Printed in the USA
CPSIA information can be obtained
at www.ICGtesting.com
CBHW071010051224
18490CB00028B/172